DREAMING THE STYX

Taking the Mystery Out of Death and Hell

SHAWN BOONSTRA

Pacific Press®
Publishing Association

Nampa, Idaho | Oshawa, Ontario, Canada
www.pacificpress.com

Cover design by Steve Lanto
Cover design resources from iStockphoto.com
Inside design by Kristin Hansen-Mellish

Illustration on page 23 source: Peter Kunzmann, Franz-Peter Burkard, and
Franz Wiedmann, *Atlas of Philosophy*, Pochothèque ed. (Paris: Le Livre de
Poche, 1993), 40, accessed July 1, 2014, http://www.agora.crosemont
.qc.ca/dphilo/intradoc/phi103/caverne.html

The author assumes full responsibility for the accuracy of all facts and
quotations as cited in this book.

You can obtain additional copies of this book by calling toll-free 1-800-765-
6955 or by visiting http://www.adventistbookcenter.com.

Library of Congress Cataloging-in-Publication Data:

Boonstra, Shawn.
  Draining the Styx : taking the mystery out of death and hell / Shawn
Boonstra.
    pages cm
  ISBN 13: 978-0-8163-5620-1 (pbk.)
  ISBN 10: 0-8163-5620-3 (pbk.)
1. Death—Biblical teaching. 2. Future life—Biblical teaching. I. Title.
BS680.L5B66 2014
236'.1—dc23

                              2014022766

June 2014

Contents

I Want to *Know* . . .

Any book on a subject as emotionally engaging as death is bound to be incomplete and thus leave the reader somewhat dissatisfied. We have been wrestling with the subject for thousands of years, yet sage philosophers and theologians still haven't exhausted the questions that can be asked. The key problem, of course, is that there aren't many people who have experienced death and can tell us what happened.

The dead don't talk.

There are some people, of course, who claim to have died and captured a glimpse of the afterlife. Bookstores almost always have one or two titles authored by supposed survivors: *Proof of Heaven*, *My Last Breath*, *The Birth Called Death*. You're almost guaranteed to find *something* on the shelf. Most of these books are the stories of people who have tiptoed up to the edge of the abyss and very briefly peeked into it. It's never for more than a few moments, and then the defibrillator suddenly jerks them back into the present world. They never actually fall into the abyss. We are remarkably short on first-person accounts by people who have been dead for several days before they come back. We have Jesus and Lazarus, of course, but none of us lives next door to someone like these two whom we can question—which means that there are limits to what a writer can say about death.

This book doesn't contain the usual first-person accounts, except in passing. Nor is it a detailed scientific analysis of death. Instead, what you are about to read is a collection of musings by a middle-aged preacher who is keenly aware of his own mortality, along with some religious history and some honest, heartfelt inquiries into what Scripture says about the subject. This book isn't meant to answer all of your questions. It is intended to start you on a journey into the subject. You will, with the rest of the human race, complete your inquiry finally and completely at a later date.

I am hoping that once you put this little book down, you will pick up another and another. I hope you will keep studying—and in particular that you'll take the time to examine what the Judeo-Christian Scripture actually says about human nature, about living, dying, and eternity. During the past two thousand years or so, folk tales and superstitions have been woven into the story. The modern thinker, then, needs to diligently distinguish these intrusions from what our ancestors actually taught.

It would be an understatement to say that our society is obsessed with death. Perhaps the reason we subject ourselves to so many violent portrayals of it on the big screen—and now on the oversized LCD screens in our family rooms—is to inoculate ourselves against our worst fear. Maybe if we see enough of it, we'll understand it more and fear it less. Of course, the opposite could be argued: the fact that most of the onscreen deaths we witness are violent, pointless, and indifferent might mean that our entertainment choices are actually worsening our dread.

It *is* interesting, nevertheless, that as we increasingly immerse ourselves in a culture of death through the entertainment industry, we spend less and less time confronting the real thing. Our ancestors—in European cultures, at any rate—used to keep the bodies of family members on display in their homes for several days before the burial, providing a close-up experience with death. Now, yesterday's wake has been reduced to a short viewing at the funeral home.

I'm hoping that as you read through this book, you'll slow down enough to ponder the topic. After all, no matter how cleverly we disguise death with silk-lined caskets and magnificent bouquets, we can't stop the inevitable: we—you as well as I—*will* die. It is well and fine for our mourners to share heartfelt stories and mournful songs, but they'll be going home, and we will still be in our caskets.

Is that blunt enough?

Personally, when it comes to death, I don't want fairy tales. As much as I enjoy a good story and the myths of ancient civilizations, I want to know what's actually going to happen when I die. From a very young age, I have noticed that death has been stalking me. I am keenly aware that my turn is coming, and when the rest of you go downstairs to the church basement for light refreshments, I will be left alone in the cold ground, waiting for a backhoe to conceal my remains.

I don't want stories. I'm standing on the bridge between youth and age, and I want to *know*. "By the sweat of your face you shall eat bread," the Bible warns us, "till you return to the ground, for out of it you were taken; for you are dust, and to dust you shall return" (Genesis 3:19).

Life is hard, and then you die. That's not just a bumper-sticker truism or an Internet meme; it's the truth.

I know the end will come, but then what?

I don't want stories. I want to *know*.

Chapter 1

Why Fight Death?

I once heard somebody say that among young people, only an unusual few think about death; but among the old, only an unusual few do not. As a kid, I was one of the unusual few. At a very young age, I seemed to be aware that I was on borrowed time.

Most guys suddenly become aware of their mortality somewhere in their late thirties to midforties, and they panic: new car, new career, new wife. Anything to assuage the fear that they have blown it—to make them feel as if there is still plenty of time left to build their dreams.

The middle-aged man looks into the mirror to discover that he is turning into his father and grandfather. The hair that used to grow near the front of his forehead is migrating to his earlobes and shoulders, and some (or much!) of what is left is turning gray. His eyes are not as bright. The days of eating an entire pizza with impunity are long gone. His waist-line has expanded over time, like a tree that adds a ring each year.

He still has an old pair of jeans in the bottom drawer of his dresser that hails from the low thirties of pant sizes. The jeans might even date all the way back to high school. If he can suck in his stomach enough to get the button done up, it quietly pops underneath the abdominal overhang when he finally exhales. He has barely used the exercise equipment in the basement. About once a year, he panics about his declining athletic ability and begins to work out. Six weeks later, he decides that his situation isn't all that bad, and he retreats back to his mediocre life, shackled to a desk under fluorescent lights forty or fifty hours a week. If he's lucky enough to work outside, his lower back and tired joints team up every morning to remind him that he's no longer a member of the track team.

He's getting old, but he refuses to admit it. He's using comb-overs, Grecian Formula dye, chemically whitened teeth—whatever it takes to fool himself into thinking that he's still young. He is, however, the *only* one who is being fooled; the general public has no problem determining his vintage.

I remember the moment when I was rudely surprised by the revelation that I was no longer considered a youth. I was on a plane flying from Los Angeles to Singapore, and a young woman, twenty-six years old, was sitting in the seat next to me. To my delight, she was a gifted conversationalist, and we had no problem running down the clock as we crossed the Pacific.

At one point, she revealed that her father taught Frisian history in a college on the East Coast.

"You're kidding!" I said. "My father was born in Friesland!" I had no idea that anybody outside of our own tribe cared to read about Friesland, let alone study it professionally.

"Listen," I said, "I'd really love to contact your father sometime. Is there some way you and I can stay in touch?"

"Well, how about e-mail?" she asked.

"No, that won't work. I almost never make it through my e-mails. There are hundreds every day."

She tried again. "What about a cell number?"

"No, same problem. I almost never answer the stupid thing."

I really wanted to contact her father. But how? Then it dawned on me: "Hey, I know! Do you have a Facebook account?"

Of course she did. Facebook had gone mainstream, and everybody was getting an account. Problem solved.

The plane had landed and pulled up to the gate, and I was standing in the aisle when it happened—when she delivered the deathblow to my youth. "You know, I'm impressed," she said. "I didn't think people your age used Facebook."

What! People my *age?*

I was horrified. I suddenly felt like the guy who is turned away at the door of an uppity restaurant for not being influential or important enough. Or the guy whose credit card is declined at the worst possible moment. I was no longer in the club. I was an *old guy.*

More serious reminders

Since that day, I've had some more serious reminders that I am speedily plowing through my life span. After the age of forty, I unexpectedly picked up a strange bug overseas that nearly took me out. I became horrifically ill, and there were a few moments when I was certain I was sitting in the departure lounge. The idea that I was mortal was no longer a theory.

I suppose the most troubling thing about life is that nobody quite knows when it will end. I have no way of knowing for sure whether I'm at the halfway point or the three-quarters point. A generation ago, lots of guys dropped dead in their sixties. Some still do. And then there are people like the otherwise healthy guy in my neighborhood who got a bad flu one Christmas and died of pneumonia in his *forties.* Nobody expected that to happen.

I have no idea when it's going to happen to me, but one thing is absolutely certain: I do have an expiry date. The problem is that nobody bothered to stamp that date on my birth certificate. Statistically, I can make an educated guess:

the Social Security Administration and insurance companies have actuary tables designed to inform them of the most likely date of my demise. There are even a few Web sites where you can plug in the date of your birth and a few other personal details and the site's computer will start counting down to a "guesstimated" date for your death in *seconds*. It's all based on averages.

I remember the first time I discovered one of those Web sites. I had a problem with my lower back stemming from an old injury; and one morning, when I was in an airport in Bucharest, my back wrenched, my legs gave out, and I dropped to the floor. I couldn't get back up, and as I lay on the floor writhing in agony, I imagined that the locals were thinking I had a bit of a drinking problem, especially since the airport bar apparently opened for business at six o'clock in the morning.

A good friend (who has since died) helped me onto a plane, and I made an excruciating trip back to Los Angeles, where an orthopedic surgeon assured me, after looking at my MRI, that if he didn't operate I stood a good chance of becoming incontinent. Up to that point, I had been resisting the idea that I might need surgery. The thought of wetting my pants uncontrollably convinced me. In fact, I pulled my Swiss Army knife out of my pocket, laid it on his desk, and told him, "You can start right now." He laughed. So did I . . . sort of.

That was Thursday. By the next Wednesday, I was on a surgical table. And when I came to, I spent the next nine weeks with a laptop in a zero-gravity lawn chair.

Before long, I felt as though I had managed to surf all the way to the end of the Internet. I'd seen it all. Incredibly bored, I snapped the computer shut and wondered what I could do to make life more interesting. *I know,* I thought, *I'll go pester the kids.*

I carefully got out of my chair, grabbed my walker, and made my way down the hallway as quietly as I could, because it was after eight o'clock. The kids were supposed to be sleeping, and I didn't want my wife, Jean, to know that I was about to disturb them.

Our youngest, Naomi, was about four or five years old, and I tried her room first. No luck; she was sound asleep. I moved on to the eight-year-old, Natalie.

When I opened the door to Natalie's room, I heard a scramble and then a click as she snapped off a flashlight. She was reading under the covers—past curfew!

"Oh, don't worry, honey," I assured her through the dark. "It's *Daddy*."

The flashlight clicked back on, and her little head poked out from under the blanket. With the flashlight illuminating her face, she looked like someone trying to tell a ghost story by a campfire.

"What do you want, Daddy?" she asked.

"Oh, nothing. I just want to hang out and talk because I'm bored."

I hobbled my way over to the edge of the bed and carefully sat down.

"What do you want to talk about?" she asked. Her eyes danced with anticipation.

"Anything!" I declared.

We both have the gift of gab, so we talked, and talked, and talked. Half an hour later, after basking in her youth, I suddenly felt a twinge of jealousy. *She's only eight,* I thought. *She still has her whole life in front of her, and she can do anything she wants. And if she's smart, she won't have to make the mistakes that I made.*

"Listen, honey," I said. "What do you want to do with your life?"

She crinkled her nose for a moment. Then she said, quite thoughtfully, "I want to be a doctor or a teacher or a mommy."

"You can do *all* those things!" I told her.

"Really?"

"Yep—you sure can. First, become a doctor. Then go back

to school and teach other doctors. And you can be a mommy too."

Natalie squirmed with excitement.

I was curious about what drove her ambition. "Why do you want to do those things?" I asked.

"I don't know. I guess I just want to *help* people."

I couldn't have been prouder. I kissed her forehead and slowly, painfully, got up to leave. When I was just about to limp my way out of her room, she suddenly continued, "And besides, Daddy, the next time you need surgery, I can do it!"

I laughed. "But Daddy's not going to need surgery for a long, long time, honey. Maybe never."

"No, that's not true!" she protested. "You're getting old! And pretty soon you're going to need a hip replacement and a knee replacement and maybe even a plate in your head!" (A plate in my head? Where in the world did she get *that*?) "And Daddy, I'll do it *all* for you!"

I went to bed that night feeling terrible. At about 2:30 in the morning, I grabbed Jean's shoulder and shook her awake.

"Honey," I said, "it's *terrible*. I've already burned through more than half a tank, and I have no idea how much is left!"

She was groggy. "What do you mean? You're not even driving yet!"

"No, not the car—*me*! I've burned through half my life. *At least* half my life—maybe more! I have no idea how much is left, and I don't even know if I lived the first half well!"

Welcome to your midlife crisis, buddy.

"Go back to sleep," Jean said. "You'll feel better in the morning."

I didn't. Not long after the sun came up, I was back online trying to figure out if other guys my age felt that way. They did. *Millions* of them. And that's when I found it: the Internet Death Clock. It's a Web site dedicated to making men's lives even more miserable. It asked for my birthday, my gender, and a few health details, and then told me, based on the national average, *exactly* how long I can expect to live as measured in seconds. And a clock popped up on the screen and started counting them down.

True, I had something like 1.8 billion seconds left, but that really isn't much. There are 3,600 seconds in an hour; 86,400 seconds in a day; and 2.5 million of them in a month. When I sat down to write this book, I went back to the Web site to check the clock and discovered that I'd already spent nearly a quarter billion of them. *A quarter billion!*

Even if I'm granted a perfectly normal, average life span, I'm running out of time faster than I want to. There are things I can do to live a bit longer—diet, exercise, careful living. But ultimately I can't put it off forever. I'm going to die.

The perfect word

Death. It's such a perfect word for what's going to happen. It starts rudely and ends with an icy whisper, sounding like someone who's hit with a blunt object and slips into unconsciousness. As you finish the word, it leaps out of your mouth, spitefully leaving the tip of your tongue trapped between your teeth. It's almost onomatopoeic.

The noted essayist Brian Jay Stanley contrasts the word *death* with one of its well-known euphemistic replacements:

> The word *death* is a strong and solid word that does not blush or flinch, calling life's terminus by its first name, without apology. But most people euphemize death with the softer phrase "passed away." To pass away suggests a gentle and painless transition from one state to another, like chilled water passing imperceptibly into ice. Thereby words conceal from our thoughts the horrors of violent accidents and the wracking agonies of terminal illness, as if everyone, instead of only a lucky few, died peacefully in their sleep. And where we peacefully pass is "away," a nebulous word that does not suggest a termination but neither does it specify a

destination. It is a kind of leaving off, a gesture of open-endedness, a set of ellipsis points at sentence's end. It is, accordingly, the perfect word for the skeptical yet sentimental modern mind, which cannot accept annihilation nor easily believe in immortality. "Passed away" allows vague hope without dogma, as if to say, "He has gone somewhere else, please don't ask for details."[1]

Create all the soft replacement words you want, but we still know exactly what you're talking about. It's still *death*. We don't like to use that word because it's too real, so we've come up with dozens—maybe hundreds—of euphemisms and dysphemisms. Some are soft, intended to mitigate the impact. Others are meant to encourage us to shrug it off with a laugh: "Buy a pine condo." "Take a dirt nap." "Assume room temperature." My favorite: "Suffered a negative patient-care outcome."

But it's hard to smile when it really happens, when you stand at the grave of someone you love after he or she has been rudely snatched away. The loss is painful, but it's also a grim reminder that we've all pulled a number out of the ticket-spitter, and there's no display on the wall of life to tell us whose number will be called next.

There is nothing I can do to avoid aging. Something in my makeup instinctively fights it, but I know that it's a battle I am guaranteed to lose. Sooner than I want, I will slip irreversibly into the dark. I fight it, but I cannot win.

Family burial plots are curious things; they sometimes display, inadvertently, an admission of defeat by a surviving spouse. Etched in the headstone next to the name of the deceased is the name of the survivor, and immediately beneath it, the date of his or her birth, followed by a dash, followed by a blank. They don't know the closing date, but they have already admitted—in stone—that it is coming. "I am waiting for you," taunts the grave.

Perhaps fortunately, my wife and I do not yet own a burial plot. We are middle-aged; we are not part of the generation that presently buys plots because we still feel too young to make such an investment. Yet even though I presently have no idea where I will be buried, my as-yet unmarked grave still calls, reminding me that I will lose the battle.

Why fight it?

What other battles do we fight in which the odds are so completely against us? Why do we stand our ground and push back when defeat is inevitable? Where does that instinct come from?

The poet Dylan Thomas wrote that we should rage against the dying of the light. I'm glad he said it, but most of us don't need a reminder. We *will* rage against it because the thought of a world that continues without us is troubling—far more troubling than the thought of a world that existed before we were born.

Why should life have to stop? The shortness of our life span seems cruel, especially when we get closer to the finish line and we realize how much we stand to lose. Why spend decades building relationships, accumulating knowledge, and learning skills, only to have your efforts suddenly come to nothing?

The wisdom acquired over a lifetime goes quietly into the grave with your body. Except for the scant few thoughts you managed to scribble down on paper, or the handful of posts and photos that survive online, everything you are and everything you believe will be lost. Nobody will be able to reassemble your thoughts or personality once you're gone. People might be able to pull together a few odds and ends and pretend that they're doing justice to your memory. There will likely be someone who knows you well enough to deliver a eulogy; but the tragic reality is that even those few imperfect recollections will fade with time because the day after you're buried, everybody else will still have to get on with their own lives.

A few years ago, my daughters gave me a couple of identical blank journals for Father's Day. I'm supposed to record something of myself in them: my likes, wishes, accomplishments, favorite memories, struggles. It's a bit like an extended résumé, just more personal. Or, for that matter, like a 128-page personal ad: "I like long walks on the beach, hiking in the mountains, classical music . . ."

It's an invitation to write my own eulogy, I suppose. There are dedicated pages for all of the usual chapters in a person's life. There's a place to trace out my family tree, a place to remember my wedding day, a place to record my travels. It's a great idea, but I have yet to complete a single page. They're all still blank. I've discovered that even *I* don't know how to adequately eulogize myself. What do I include? What do I leave out? What will seem important to my children when I am dead?

The empty journals mock me like my empty grave: "Not only are you going to die, but there's no conceivable way to express yourself in a way that will convey how important your life was to you. And even if you could, nobody outside of your own family would care."

I've come to feel as though filling in those pages would be like signing my own death certificate. Those journals are designed to be enjoyed when I am *dead*. I know it's coming, but do I have to commit to it on paper?

I suppose I should suck it up and start on them while I still have time to think things through. If I leave it too long, I'll be cramming for finals, making a hasty attempt to scribble a few things down when the final chimes are sounding and they're keeping me from thinking clearly. It's like packing for a long trip. If I leave it to the last minute, I'm going to forget a lot of important stuff.

But if I fail to record *something* for my kids, there will soon be little left of me when I'm gone—just a few sandy memories being steadily eroded by the ebb and flow of time. And when my own children eventually succumb to the same fate, *all* memory of me will be lost. I will be merely another headstone in a graveyard. Most of the passersby won't stop long enough to read my name; and if they do, it will be meaningless. I will be two dates etched in stone; the first one meant something only to my parents, the second one to my wife and children.

But let's suppose that for some reason my name did mean something. Suppose that I managed to accomplish something legendary or notorious before I died. Let's suppose everybody knew my name. What good is that? I will never know that they know it, and whatever they think they know about me will be flawed and incomplete. Their impression of who I was won't be shaped by my influence but by the words of people who merely presume to understand who I was.

Is there anything crueler? To build a life, to deepen relationships, to acquire knowledge and wisdom and skills—and then to have death take it all, irrevocably.

So why bother? Why struggle? Why push back against the Reaper when he arrives? What is it that makes us want to survive?

Why, when death is inevitable, do we still feel cheated when it comes?

Endnote

1. Brian Jay Stanley, "On the Phrase 'Passed Away,' " *Aphorisms and Paradoxes* (blog), http://www.brianjaystanley.com/aphorisms /on-the-phrase-passed-away.

Interlude

The Middle-Aged Lollipop

I was busy conquering my fourth mile when I saw it: a half-melted lollipop stuck to the sidewalk. I had no idea that lollipops could melt. Of course, sugar *does* melt in a pan over a flame. But on the sidewalk in Ventura, California? I didn't expect it, especially in the mild temperatures of a summer tempered by cool winds off the Pacific Ocean. Obviously, the sidewalk had become hot enough the day before to begin the sticky process of liquefaction.

The curious thing was how the candy had been *half* melted. It looked like an ice cream cone that had been dropped just moments ago. It retained most of its original shape, except for a puddle of green that had formed around the edges, as if someone had pushed the pause button halfway through the witch's demise in *The Wizard of Oz*. Was it dropped in the evening, just as the air cooled enough to stop the process? Had sunset saved a disfigured treat from annihilation?

A few years ago, I wouldn't have noticed a lollipop on the

sidewalk except to become irritated at the thoughtless person who dropped it and failed to pick it up. But that morning I was thinking about this book—about death and my own deepening sense of mortality. I thought maybe middle-aged guys are like that lollipop. Somewhere past the age of forty, life drops you on the ground and you begin to dissolve. You retain much of your original shape, but parts of you begin to ooze out on the hot concrete: your eyesight, your lower back, your adrenaline and testosterone. Kidneys that used to put up with all manner of abuse suddenly make stones. Skin that was once smooth begins to sprout unwanted hair. A tooth breaks. A knee rips. Wounds take longer to heal.

It happens rather suddenly. One moment you feel perfectly fine, unaware that you are teetering dangerously close to the edge of your youth—and then you suddenly fall and hit the sidewalk. It hurts, and you begin to ooze. The heat cooks your dreams out of you, making you wonder if you've made the right decisions in life, if you've had the right priorities. You can't believe how quickly you're dissolving.

And then it stops. Somehow, the sun goes down, the sidewalk cools, and the decay slows and stops, leaving you mostly intact. It brings a sense of relief: I am *not* dying. But the memory of how quickly the first round of deterioration began will haunt you. You know the sun will rise, the sidewalk will heat up again, and your annihilation will resume.

Nobody makes it past the second day. There are graveyards full of people to prove that.

Chapter 2

Dead Bodies, Living Spirits?

Maybe I'm being too pessimistic. Perhaps death isn't a cheat and a thief. Maybe it is a friend. I've been to a lot of funerals, after all, where death has been presented as if it's a graduation: "He's in a better place now."

That claim raises an important question. If death really takes us to a better place, why fight against dying? Why the instinct to avoid it?

According to Plato, when the Greek philosopher Socrates was condemned to death for supposedly corrupting the youth of Athens, he *didn't* fight it. Most first-year philosophy students are required to read Plato's account. Socrates is one of history's great non-Christian martyrs. Because of this, some people have compared the deaths of Jesus and Socrates. However, the stark contrasts between the two are more significant than the similarities. Primarily, nobody thought of Socrates as the human incarnation of God. But the parallel is useful to a discussion about death nonetheless.

Socrates was executed by poisoning. The curious thing

about the story is that nobody held him down and forced the poison into him; he was given a brew made from *Conium maculatum,* poison hemlock, and he drank it willingly. He was executed by the state, but he participated in the process cheerfully.

Why? Why didn't he pinch his lips together, refuse the poison, and fight to the last?

There are at least two answers to that question. Socrates believed that because he was content to live as a citizen of Athens, he couldn't justify running away from the verdict that he was guilty of breaking the laws of the city. His friends actually pleaded with him to make his escape, but he refused. It was a matter of principle; he died willingly because he believed in the importance of his city-state's government. So in one respect, he died willingly because he was an idealist who sacrificed himself to principle.

But there is another reason, one that is far more profound. Pay attention to the fact that Socrates was a *Greek* philosopher, and the Greeks were dualists.

What is dualism? Plato—a student of Socrates and the man who recorded Socrates's final moments for us—is perhaps the most suitable person to explain it. He taught something known to modern students of philosophy as the theory of forms, which illustrates dualism nicely. It runs something like this:

1. It is obvious that the world around us, and everything in it, is flawed. Careful examination shows that nothing is perfect. You can always find mistakes and imperfections.
2. But how do we *know* when something is imperfect? For us to consider something as imperfect, we must have some idea of what the perfect is.
3. And if we can conceive of perfection, it must exist—there must be a realm of perfection somewhere in this universe. That realm must be a

nonmaterial world of *ideals*. Everything we see in
the material world is but a dim shadow of its perfect counterpart in the nonmaterial world.

My description is a little simplistic, and it probably wouldn't
get much more than a C- from my philosophy professors, but in
a nutshell, that's it. In perhaps Plato's most famous explanation of
the concept, he likened us to prisoners who are sitting in a cave
and staring at its back wall. There's a fire behind us, and occasionally, some-one or something passes between the fire and us, casting a shadow on the wall in front of us. We know nothing of this thing other than what we can see in its shadow. The shadows are not reality; they are only the *form* of something real. We cannot actually see the real world be-cause we're turned in the wrong direc-tion. But if we

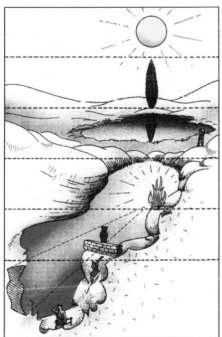

study the shadows long enough, we can begin to learn things
about the real physical objects that cast those shadows.

Studying the shadows is the job of the philosopher. With
careful thought and study, there is much to be learned about
the higher world that produces the shadows. But regardless of
how intelligent we might be, we're still shackled in the cave,

doomed to examine the reality of the universe by examining silhouettes on the wall.

Greek dualism is so-called because of the belief in two realms of existence: our imperfect material world that is the shadow, and the perfect immaterial world that exists somewhere above our plane of existence.

What does this have to do with death? Plenty. Your body is part of the material world, the realm of shadows. You don't have to live on this planet for long to discover the many imperfections that come with a physical human body. But how do we know when something is malfunctioning? How do we recognize imperfection? Is there a greater, more perfect reality somewhere on the higher planes of the immaterial universe than human existence on this planet? Is it possible that we have a nonmaterial *soul* in addition to a material body?

The birth of ghosts

Questions like those above led to the belief in ghosts. Of course, the Greeks cannot lay sole claim to the discovery; ghosts were an integral part of most ancient pagan cultures. But the Greeks *did* popularize them and made them part of the thought processes of the intellectual elites.

In the minds of both Socrates and his student Plato, the purpose of philosophy was to explore the higher realms even though the philosophers were among those trapped in the cave, in the prison-house of a human body. Some practiced asceticism—denying themselves the enjoyment of worldly pleasure. They abstained to keep their bodies, and thus their minds, pure enough for philosophical pursuits. They beat their bodies into subjection so they could move more confidently toward the day when they would finally be released from the imperfect material cave to see the immaterial "real world."

Here, in rather tedious language, is how Plato described someone attempting to escape the material world by denying the body and studying philosophy:

Only the philosopher who departs pure is permitted to enter the company of the gods. This is the reason why he abstains from fleshly lusts, and not because he fears loss or disgrace, which is the motive of other men. He too has been a captive, and the willing agent of his own captivity. But philosophy has spoken to him, and he has heard her voice; she has gently entreated him, and brought him out of the "miry clay," and purged away the mists of passion and the illusions of sense which envelope him; his soul has escaped from the influence of pleasures and pains, which are like nails fastening her to the body. To that prison-house she will not return; and therefore she abstains from bodily pleasures—not from a desire of having more or greater ones, but because she knows that only when calm and free from the dominion of the body can she behold the light of truth.[1]

So, Plato argued (by putting words in Socrates's mouth), if you don't break free from worldly lust and material passions, you will never embrace death as the gift that it is. You'll be afraid to die. You'll be hesitant to leave this world.

It was because Socrates was a philosopher that he wasn't afraid to die. He believed death would be a treat: the long-awaited release from the prison of his material body. He thought he would finally get to step out of the cave and see the *real* universe and all the things that had been casting shadows on this world.

Since he had that understanding of death, it's easy to understand why he told his friends to stop crying. He wasn't about to lose his life; he was about to graduate.

Socrates's positive attitude toward death has survived the centuries. To this day, it can be found in the funerals of Western civilization: "Don't cry—he's in a better place."

Our poetry often echoes Socrates's desire to die:

Vital spark of heav'nly flame,
Quit, oh, quit this mortal frame!
Trembling, hoping, ling'ring, flying,
Oh, the pain, the bliss of dying!
Cease, fond Nature, cease thy strife,
And let me languish into life!
(Alexander Pope, "The Dying Christian
to His Soul")

Friend or foe?

Given the obvious horrors of death, Plato's philosophy provides an undeniable level of comfort: death is not the end, it is the beginning. It is a graduation—a liberation. It makes perfect sense to adopt this philosophy as a coping mechanism, but something that noted Lutheran theologian Oscar Cullmann pointed out back in the 1950s makes me hesitant: Socrates might have thought of death as a friend, but Jesus certainly didn't.

> Plato shows us how Socrates goes to his death in complete peace and composure. The death of Socrates is a beautiful death. Nothing is seen here of death's terror. Socrates cannot fear death, since indeed it sets us free from the body. Whoever fears death proves that he loves the world of the body, that he is thoroughly entangled in the world of sense. Death is the soul's great friend. . . .
>
> And now let us hear how Jesus dies. In Gethsemane He knows that death stands before Him, just as Socrates expected death on his last day. . . . Jesus begins "to tremble and be distressed," writes Mark (14:33). "My soul is troubled, even to death," He says to His disciples. . . . Jesus is afraid, though not as a coward would be of the men who will kill Him, still less of the pain and grief which precede death. He is afraid in the face of death itself. Death

for Him is not something divine: it is something dreadful. Jesus does not want to be alone in this moment. He knows, of course, that the Father stands by to help Him. He looks to Him in this decisive moment as He has done throughout His life. He turns to Him with all His human fear of this great enemy, death. He is afraid of death. It is useless to try to explain away Jesus' fear as reported by the Evangelists. The opponents of Christianity who already in the first centuries made the contrast between the death of Socrates and the death of Jesus saw more clearly here than the exponents of Christianity. He was really afraid. Here is nothing of the composure of Socrates, who met death peacefully as a friend. . . . Now, when God's enemy stands before Him, He cries to God, whose omnipotence He knows: "All things are possible with thee; let this cup pass from me" (Mark 14:36).[2]

You've got to admit, he has a powerful point: Jesus didn't embrace death at all. He submitted to it for the sake of the human race. He resigned Himself to it. He struggled profoundly in the face of it, but He didn't love it as Socrates did.

And He was withdrawn from them about a stone's throw, and He knelt down and prayed, saying, "Father, if it is Your will, take this cup away from Me; nevertheless, not My will, but Yours be done." Then an angel appeared to Him from heaven, strengthening Him. And being in agony, He prayed more earnestly. Then His sweat became like great drops of blood falling down to the ground (Luke 22:41–44).

Christians and those of us raised in the Christian world should be asking why there is such a sharp contrast between Jesus and Socrates. Why didn't Jesus cling to the same ethereal hopes as the great philosopher? Why not embrace the hope that death would be a sweet release from the painful existence of this world—the idea that His execution was merely a ticket to the next level up?

What did Jesus know that Socrates didn't?

I suppose someone could argue that Jesus was a humble carpenter who wasn't privy to the wealth of philosophy that Socrates had, so His fear was born of ignorance. For Christians, that is an unacceptable explanation; but if Socrates had been around, he might have suggested it. "He's afraid because He doesn't understand. He didn't manage to use His mind to break free from the material world before now, so He's afraid to let go of this place." Plato's account reveals that this is essentially what Socrates said about anybody who feared death. But nobody who has read the Bible would believe that about Jesus. His agony doesn't come from ignorance; it is born of profound knowledge. Jesus *knows* something about the subject.

"Do not be afraid," Jesus says in the first chapter of the book of Revelation. "I am the First and the Last. I am He who lives, and was dead, and behold, I am alive forevermore. Amen. And I have the keys of Hades and of Death" (Revelation 1:17, 18). Jesus not only knows something about death; He claims to have conquered it and to hold the keys to its imprisonment.

Every thoughtful Westerner ought to have a careful look at the stark difference between Socrates and Jesus. Theologian Oscar Cullmann gave the topic very careful consideration, and it brought him to some conclusions that landed him in hot water with other theologians. What Cullmann pointed out doesn't blend easily with the eulogies and sermons of modern Christian funerals. If we admit that Jesus was uncomfortable in the face of death, how can we ask Christians to be OK with it? And if Cullmann is right, aren't we robbing people of hope when they need it most?

" 'Has M. Cullmann,' " one of his critics wrote, " 'a stone instead of a heart?' "[3]

I don't believe for a moment that he did. He was asking a valid question. Why did Jesus hate death? Why did He cry at the tomb of His friend Lazarus (John 11:35)? If death is a release from suffering, an upgrade to a better mode of existence, then why do we fight it? Why is there still an alarm bell in our minds, convincing us that it is *not* OK? Why do we all seem to fight death, and rage against it when it comes?

The nihilist's graveside tree

A few years ago, my good friend Cliff called me and asked if I had seen the funeral service for Douglas Adams, which apparently had been posted on the BBC's Web site.

"No," I replied, "I haven't."

"You should," he told me, "because they did something really interesting at his grave."

"What's that?" I asked, not sure I'd have time to look it up.

"They planted a tree!"

There's nothing terribly unusual about that, of course. Lots of people plant trees on or near burial plots. But in this case, it was an interesting thing to do. You wouldn't think that the mourners at Douglas Adams's funeral would find any significance in the symbolism usually attached to such an act, because many, if not most of them, were skeptics. Atheists, in fact. Adams himself was a nihilist—someone who doesn't believe that life has meaning. A nihilist believes that there's no particular reason or purpose for our existence. A nihilist approach to death would be quite different from that of Plato or Socrates. Nihilists don't expect to move up to (or *down* to, for that matter) another plane of existence. They don't expect to go anywhere at all.

Adams's views became popularized through his best-known work, *The Hitchhiker's Guide to the Galaxy.* It started out as a series of quirky radio shows produced in the late 1970s, which he later turned into a book, and more recently a movie. At one point in the story, readers (or viewers) are told about a race of highly intelligent beings that, in the ancient past, designed a supercomputer named Deep Thought to enable them to discover the meaning of life. They asked Deep Thought to calculate the answer to the ultimate question "of life, the universe and everything."[4]

The computer worked on the problem for 7.5 million years and then gave an unusual answer: "Forty-two." The computer then pointed out that the answer is meaningless because the programmers never actually knew the question to ask in the first place. It then suggests that it might be able to help build an even better computer—one that could give them the question that would produce a meaningful answer. But those plans are ultimately derailed, and the audience is told that the question and the answer cannot both exist in the same universe.

This radio show, book, and movie weren't just a bit of science-fiction fun. Adams was making a point: our existence is purposeless. You don't really mean *anything*. Forty-two is just as good an answer to the question of the meaning of life as anything else.

Planting a tree on Adams's grave was an interesting thing to do. What kind of comfort can a skeptic or a nihilist bring to a funeral? Why in the world would someone plant a tree? People usually plant trees on graves because trees are a symbol of life. People plant trees to demonstrate hope, to force some remnant of a person to continue after he or she has died. They plant trees because every fiber of their being is screaming that death is a thief, and that something is profoundly wrong with our coming to such a sudden end. They plant trees in defiance of mortality.

But if you're a nihilist, it makes no sense. Not if you believe there is absolutely nothing past the grave.

Our brains tell us that we're going to die. When we're young, it's merely a fact that we glean from the conversations of the elderly or the actuary tables of the insurance company. Statistically, we're all going to die. Nobody escapes the grave.

Intellectually, we *know* that. And if we believe that life on earth is merely an accident, the product of a very long string of coincidences and random fortuitous events and conditions, that should be all there is to the discussion: you live and you die, and that's it. Case closed. But no matter how much our logic tells us that death is a fact of existence, there is something in our hearts that screams against it when it approaches. Even though death is perfectly fair in that it takes every one of us, and even though we know there is ultimately no way to prevent it, we still feel cheated when it happens. We push back. Something tells us that death is *wrong*.

Where in the world does *that* instinct come from? If death is inevitable, and our lives are just more random occurrences in a long string of biological happenings on an insignificant planet on the edge of an unremarkable spiral galaxy, why fight it? Why not simply shrug when your number is called and quietly go to your destiny?

And why bother to plant a tree on a grave? It seems kind of pointless.

Unless even a hardened skeptic can still feel the sentiment of Jesus when it comes to mortality. There's something horribly *wrong* with it.

Another garden hints at hope

We might find wisdom at the Taj Mahal, which is, in my humble opinion, one of the few tourist attractions on this planet that actually lives up to its reputation. I can't tell you how often I've gone to see some well-known destination, only to be sharply disappointed by the divergence between the spectacular photos in the travel brochure and the somewhat downgraded reality of the place. But the Taj Mahal is different; it's easily one of the most stunning structures on the planet.

The marble sepulcher was built in the seventeenth century by Shah Jahan, the Mughal emperor, as a memorial to his third wife, Mumtaz Mahal. She died giving birth to their fourteenth child, and, as the story goes, the emperor was so grief-stricken that he considered suicide. Rather than take his own life, however, he decided to build a spectacular tomb for the woman he loved. It is perhaps the world's most spectacular monument to grief.

What I find most interesting is not the tomb itself but the garden immediately in front of it. If you've ever seen a picture of the Taj Mahal, you've seen the garden—or at least part of it. Most photographers stand at the far end of the garden in order to catch a reflection of the tomb in the pools that stretch across the grounds.

The garden is roughly square, and there's a pool at its center from which four walkways and canals run to the edges of the garden, dividing it into four smaller squares. The design of the garden is based on some very old ideas. The Moguls borrowed the design from the ancient Persians, who, rather prosaically, called it "Walled Enclosure." In Persian, the term used to name such a garden is a compound word, which the Persians borrowed from the Medes. The two words that form the compound are *pairi,* which means "around," and *daeza,* which means "wall." The garden is literally an "around wall," or *pairi-daeza.* From that compound we get the word *paradise.* The basic design of the Taj Mahal garden, then, is a "paradise garden."

This design deliberately hearkens back to the biblical story of the Garden of Eden. The garden pictured in Genesis was a paradise from which four rivers flowed and in the midst of which stood the tree of life. When Adam and Eve sinned and became subject to death, they were escorted out of the Garden to live the rest of their lives in hardship. A pair of cherubim were stationed at the gates of the Garden "to guard the way to the tree of life" (Genesis 3:24). Sinful human beings could not be permitted to live forever; there was no telling what depths of depravity and suffering they might be capable of, given unlimited time.

By sinning, the human race drove a sharp wedge between

themselves and their life-giving, holy Creator, because of which they would die. But they would not die without hope. Before escorting Adam and Eve out of the Garden to experience the miserable world they'd made for themselves, God gave them a promise: the Seed of the woman would come to pay for their sins and reverse their fortunes (verse 15). This was the first Messianic promise, a prophecy of the God-man who would come to save the human race. The promise meant that the expulsion of human beings from the Garden wasn't permanent. The angels weren't primarily *barring* the way to the tree of life; they were *guarding* that tree. Eventually, the path would be reopened, and the human race would be read-mitted to paradise. Death would be reversed. In fact, the Bible ends on that very note:

> He showed me a pure river of water of life, clear as crystal, proceeding from the throne of God and of the Lamb. In the middle of its street, and on either side of the river, was the tree of life, which bore twelve fruits, each tree yielding its fruit every month. The leaves of the tree were for the healing of the nations (Revelation 22:1, 2).

The layout of the paradise garden at the Taj Mahal—and other paradise gardens like it—was meant to serve as a tangible reminder of God's promise that death need not be forever. God made the promise just outside the edge of the Garden, where Adam and Eve would die. Just outside the perimeter of the paradise garden at the Taj Mahal is another painful monument to suffering and death. But it sits *adjacent* to paradise, so it becomes a symbol of hope——hope that access to the garden has not been cut off forever.

But why go through the trouble of constructing an elaborate memorial if there *is* no hope? Why resist? Why not simply admit defeat and get on with life?

We resist death because we are profoundly hardwired to

do so. We are born with—and live with—an instinct that tells us we're being cheated by death, that there's something wrong with the current order of things.

Even if you happen to believe that the Garden of Eden is a myth (I do not), you still have to ask yourself why ancient people would go to such trouble to try to explain suffering and death. Why bother constructing a story to explain *why* we die? Wouldn't it be simpler to just admit that we die and that's that?

Except, we *don't*. We have a profound need to understand *why* we die. We demand to know why our existence, in the words of Thomas Hobbes, is "nasty, brutish and short." We struggle with a deep sense of having been cheated, a sense that something is terribly wrong.

Even if Eden *were* a myth, we would have to ask ourselves why we need such a myth.

Perhaps Socrates was the one who had it wrong. Perhaps Jesus had it right: death is *not* a friend; it's an intruder whose cruel presence demands an explanation. Jesus looked into the darkness of death and He trembled. According to Christian understanding, He wasn't facing merely His own death, He was facing yours as well. He was your substitute, giving His life as a ransom for many (Matthew 20:28), becoming sin for you (2 Corinthians 5:21), and thus receiving your death, the wages of *your* sin (Romans 6:23; cf. Isaiah 53:4, 5; 1 Peter 3:18).

No wonder He trembled.

Socrates embraced death like someone getting an upgrade to first class. Jesus faced it for what it truly is: our enemy (1 Corinthians 15:26). It is *not* part of God's design. Those who feel the need to plant trees on graves are unwittingly underscoring the Bible's assertion.

Of course, we still have to explain why the modern Christian funeral often sounds more like Socrates than Jesus. You are more likely to hear a preacher say that the deceased has moved on to a better experience than to hear him or her weep and tremble in the horrible face of death.

The smooth, reassuring language we sometimes hear at gravesides seems more like something from Athens than from Gethsemane—a rather strange situation, because the New Testament doesn't advise us to comfort each other with talk about ascending to higher realms. It speaks of something else: a different hope, a better hope.

Endnotes

1. Plato, *Phaedo,* trans. Benjamin Jowett, iBooks ed., iBooks location 14/266.

2. Oscar Cullmann, "The Last Enemy," in *Immortality of the Soul or Resurrection of the Dead?* Translated from "Mélanges offerts à KARL BARTH à l'occasion de ses 70 ans," in *Theologische Zeitschrift* 2, 126ff. (1956), http://www.religion-online.org/showchapter.asp?title=1115&C=1215.

3. Cullman, preface to *Immortality of the Soul,* http://www.religion-online.org/showchapter.asp?title=1115&C=1213.

4. Douglas Adams, *The Hitchhiker's Guide to the Galaxy* (New York: Harmony Books, 1979), 182.

Chapter 3

The Bible on Death

Before we begin to study how the hope of New Testament Christianity differed from that of ancient Athens, we should examine the subject of death itself as it's presented in the Bible. I have to warn you, though, that when you collect all of the relevant biblical data and you jettison the mythology that two thousand years of Western civilization has heaped on the subject, it can be a little disorienting. The complete picture sometimes comes as a surprise to people who haven't seen it before.

Perhaps the best place to start is in Eden. The opening chapters of Genesis record the origin of human life. If you want to understand how life ends, it's important that you grasp how it began. Life is, after all, a bigger mystery than death. We struggle to explain it. We can describe the chemical processes that keep us ticking from day to day, right down to the cellular level, but we're not entirely sure what life actually *is*. What makes us self-aware and conscious? What is the spark that actually gives us life?

The biblical account of human origins is remarkably simple: "The Lord God formed man of the dust of the ground, and breathed into his nostrils the breath of life; and man became a living being" (Genesis 2:7).

We are carbon-based life-forms. My eighth-grade biology

teacher said that, essentially, we're "made of the same stuff you find in your chimney." Though he was not a believer, that teacher might have been surprised to discover that basically he was agreeing with the author of Genesis, who tells us that human beings were made from the "dust of the ground."

That much we understand: we are made of the same chemical elements as the ones that make up the earth and all that's found on it. What we *don't* understand is this: How do inorganic elements become walking, talking, sentient beings with distinct personalities? How does a collection of chemicals laugh, cry, hate, and love? How can someone make you and me from a pile of dirt?

The Bible writers present God as the One who provided the spark of life, the One who breathed into Adam's nostrils "the breath of life." The same idea can be found in Paul's letter to the church in Colossae, albeit indirectly. Speaking of Jesus, whom the Bible says is God incarnate, Paul writes,

> He is the image of the invisible God, the firstborn over all creation. For by Him all things were created that are in heaven and that are on earth, visible and invisible, whether thrones or dominions or principalities or powers. All things were created through Him and for Him. And He is before all things, and in Him all things consist (Colossians 1:15–17).

In describing Jesus, Paul tells us essentially the same thing as we read in Genesis: God is the One who provides the spark of life. Not only did He make everything but "in Him all things consist." Nothing, including us, could exist without Him. Elements do not love or laugh without the divine spark.

So, according to the biblical account, the formula for life is simple:

> Dust of the ground + the breath of life (the God-given spark) = a living being

The biblical formula for death is just a reversal of the formula for life:

Dust of the ground − the breath of life (the God-given spark) = a dead being

David put it this way: "You hide Your face, they are troubled; You take away their breath, they die and return to their dust" (Psalm 104:29). Genesis says much the same: "By the sweat of your face you shall eat bread, till you return to the ground, for out of it you were taken; for you are dust, and to dust you shall return" (Genesis 3:19). And the book of Ecclesiastes says something similar, but with a small twist: "The dust will return to the earth as it was, and the spirit will return to God who gave it" (Ecclesiastes 12:7).

At this point some confusion starts to build. Just what is the "spirit" that goes back to God?

Spirit and breath

Socrates expected to leave his body and ascend to a better existence, and the author of Ecclesiastes *seems* to be saying the same thing—that our bodies turn to dust and our "spirits" head for the higher realms, to be in the presence of God. But in the language in which Genesis was written, that's not quite what the verse is saying. The Hebrew word that has been translated "spirit" in English is *ruach*. This word can actually mean several things—*wind, breath, mind,* and *spirit* among them. But the primary sense of the word is simply "breath." That's why, in the old King James Version, you find this odd passage in the book of Job: "All the while my breath is in me, and the spirit of God is in my nostrils" (Job 27:3, KJV).

Was Job actually telling us that the Spirit of God was living in his nostrils?

No.

The word translated "spirit" here is *ruach*, which, as we've noted, can also mean "breath." If we take it to mean some sort of disembodied ghost, we run into a ridiculous assertion: Job had a ghost up his nose. The ancient Hebrews often communicated their thoughts through parallel assertions, a pattern that is especially frequent in the book of Psalms. In this case, Job's expressions, "the breath that is in me" and "the spirit of God that is in my nostrils," mean the same thing. It's the same thought delivered twice. Job is acknowledging that his ability to breathe—in other words, to live—is a gift that only God can give. When God withdraws that gift, we stop breathing, and then we die.

That's the same thing the author of Ecclesiastes was saying: the dust returns to the earth, and the spirit—the breath— returns to God. In fact, in the *New American Standard Bible,* the translators went to the trouble of creating a marginal note to let us know that "spirit" can be translated "breath"—and for the sake of our modern Western minds, probably should have been translated that way in this case. Ecclesiastes is saying the same thing that Genesis, Colossians, and Psalms say: When you live, it is because God has granted the gift of life. When that gift is gone, you stop breathing and turn back into dust.

This sheds great light on why the "wages of sin is death" (Romans 6:23). Our sins separate us from God (Isaiah 59:2). They drive a wedge between the Creator and His creatures, and that compromises the connection we have with our Source of life. A world untethered from its Source of life is a world that unravels. Beings that are disconnected from the Source of life are living on borrowed time. Unplug a fan, and inertia may keep the blades spinning for a little while, but you know they will stop. A car with a leaky fuel line will struggle to keep going for long. And human beings who sin may coast through a short existence, but they, too, will die.

Of course, this isn't the picture that was presented to me growing up. I was told that the spirit was my *ghost,* and that when I died, my "spirit" would immediately go to be with God. My body was just a shell in which my spirit lived for a time, and once my body was gone, I would live more freely. But that idea, as prevalent as it has become in Western society, is at odds with the picture actually given in the Bible. It's a concept that seems more likely to have come from Socrates than from the biblical psalmist, who quite clearly emphasized that we do *not* move to another conscious existence when we die:

> While I live I will praise the LORD; I will sing praises to my God while I have my being. Do not put your trust in princes, nor in a son of man, in whom there is no help. His spirit departs, he returns to his earth; in that very day his plans perish (Psalm 146:2–4).

The word translated "plans" is *'eshtonah,* which literally means "thought." Some of the more literal translations, such as the *New American Standard Bible* and the King James Version, translate the verse to say "in that very day his *thoughts* perish." This is, of course, what some of the less literal translations say: your thoughts come to a screeching halt the moment you die, and by extension, so do all of your plans.

In other words, when you die, your conscious existence—your whole life—ends.

No praise from the dead

Think about this carefully for a moment: as a Christian, I absolutely plan to be with God after I die, and yet the Bible says that all of my plans, all of my thoughts stop the moment I expire. I can assure you that if I were suddenly whisked into the presence of God at the moment of death, I'd be having *some* thoughts: *I can't believe I'm here!* But the psalmist expected no such thing; he declared that it *all* stops the moment I die. And he says it more than once. Note, for instance, Psalm 115:17: "The dead do not praise the LORD, nor any who go down into silence."

Of course, that flies right in the face of what I was told as a kid. I was told then that if I died, I'd immediately join the choirs in heaven.

No such luck. According to the Bible, dead people do *not*

praise God. The Bible says this again and again. Here's another instance: "As the cloud disappears and vanishes away, so he who goes down to the grave does not come up. He shall never return to his house, nor shall his place know him anymore" (Job 7:9, 10).

So much for the dead returning to haunt their homes! The Bible says they are forever disconnected from life on this earth—which of course makes you wonder what was actually happening that made people claim that someone was visiting them from beyond the grave. According to the Bible, that someone isn't a dead relative, which raises the chilling question of *who else* could be this apparition that disappears like a cloud evaporating into the atmosphere.* Here are a couple more biblical texts on the topic:

- "The living know that they will die; but *the dead know nothing,* and they have no more reward, for the memory of them is forgotten. Also *their love, their hatred, and their envy have now perished; nevermore will they have a share in anything done under the sun*" (Ecclesiastes 9:5, 6; emphasis added).
- "Whatever your hand finds to do, do it with your might; for *there is no work or device or knowledge or wisdom in the grave where you are going*" (Ecclesiastes 9:10; emphasis added).

Admittedly, it's a bleak picture. When you're dead, *you're dead.* You don't praise God, you are silent, your plans and thoughts perish, your wisdom is gone, and you never again have anything to do with life under the sun. It comes as a

---

* Some people far too quickly dismiss such reports as the figment of someone's imagination. I have seen enough over the years to keep me from dismissing every such report. Some people really *do* experience strange things—there's just no getting around it. From a biblical perspective, however, I know it cannot be the ghost of a dead loved one.

surprise to many people who have been reared in the Judeo-Christian tradition that the Old Testament says nothing about an ethereal afterlife. Nowhere do you find a record of people who are whisked off to heaven at the time of death. *There are no ghosts.**

Apparently, Socrates either wasn't familiar with the Hebrew Scriptures or he didn't believe them. Plato has him defending the idea of an immaterial, immortal soul at length; but no such defense is found from the authors of the Bible. In fact, there is only a single reference to an immortal being to be found in the Bible, and this Being is not human. He is "the King of kings and Lord of lords, who *alone* has immortality, dwelling in unapproachable light, whom no man has seen or can see, to whom be honor and everlasting power. Amen" (1 Timothy 6:15, 16; emphasis added).

Of all the beings in the universe, only God possesses natural immortality. Human beings had immortality before they sinned, but it was reliant on God. The moment human beings sinned, they no longer had it.

Of course, that doesn't mean there is *nothing* after death. A few verses earlier, Paul was encouraging Timothy to "lay hold on eternal life" (verse 12), so we know that the Christian's talk of living forever *does* have a basis in Scripture. We *do* have hope. It's just that our hope is not found *in* death, because death is exactly what it sounds like: the complete absence of life. Our hope comes *after* the grave, at a time when death will be reversed.

Like sleep

Perhaps you've noticed that the Bible writers' favorite metaphor for death is sleep. You'll find that comparison made no fewer than fifty times. Jesus Himself made this comparison when His good friend Lazarus died. The Bible story about

---

* The one exception, of course, is the apparition at Endor. We shall visit that in due time.

that incident is worth reproducing at length because it sheds so much light on the Bible's understanding of death.

Lazarus had become ill, and his sisters sent someone to tell Jesus, expecting that Jesus would immediately drop what He was doing and head to Bethany, Lazarus's hometown, and heal him as He had so many other people.

But Jesus didn't do what they expected Him to do. In fact, He stayed where He was for two more days. When He finally started out for Bethany, Scripture says He told His disciples, " 'Our friend Lazarus sleeps, but I go that I may wake him up.' Then His disciples said, 'Lord, if he sleeps he will get well.' However, Jesus spoke of his death, but they thought that He was speaking about taking rest in sleep" (John 11:11–13).

Jesus couldn't have stated more clearly His understanding of death. It isn't a higher existence; it's more like sleep.

As Jesus approaches the house where mourners have already gathered, Lazarus's sister Martha runs out to meet Him, and the dialogue that takes place then may be some of the clearest in the Bible on the topics of death, dying, and eternal life. Pay close attention:

> Now Martha, as soon as she heard that Jesus was coming, went and met Him, but Mary was sitting in the house. Now Martha said to Jesus, "Lord, if You had been here, my brother would not have died. But even now I know that whatever You ask of God, God will give You."
>
> Jesus said to her, "Your brother will rise again."
>
> Martha said to Him, "I know that he will rise again in the resurrection at the last day" (verses 20–24).

Notice what Jesus *doesn't* say. He doesn't tell Martha that her brother is in a better place, or that his ghost is presently in heaven. If Jesus believed those things to be true, you'd expect

Him to express such happy thoughts at a moment when they would have been useful: "Don't worry, Martha; he's in a better place. He's in heaven with My Father."

But Jesus doesn't say that. He doesn't talk about altered existence. Instead, He mentions a *future* existence: "Your brother will rise again, Martha."

And she replies, "I know. In the resurrection, at the last day."

Oops. Martha apparently wasn't reading Plato. There is the promise of a future life, but for now, Lazarus is dead. He sleeps. He isn't conscious of anything. But at some point in the future, at the Second Coming, the graves will be opened, and Lazarus will come back to life. That's the description of death presented everywhere in the Bible:

- "At that time Michael shall stand up, the great prince who stands watch over the sons of your people; and there shall be a time of trouble, such as never was since there was a nation, even to that time. And at that time your people shall be delivered, everyone who is found written in the book. And many of those who sleep in the dust of the earth shall awake, some to everlasting life, some to shame and everlasting contempt" (Daniel 12:1, 2).

- "Most assuredly, I say to you, the hour is coming, and now is, when the dead will hear the voice of the Son of God; and those who hear will live. For as the Father has life in Himself, so He has granted the Son to have life in Himself, and has given Him authority to execute judgment also, because He is the Son of man. Do not marvel at this; for the hour is coming in which all who are in the graves will hear His voice and come forth—those who have done good, to the resurrection of life, and those who have done evil, to the resurrection of condemnation" (John 5:25–29).

- "For the Lord Himself will descend from heaven

with a shout, with the voice of an archangel, and with the trumpet of God. And the dead in Christ will rise first. Then we who are alive and remain shall be caught up together with them in the clouds to meet the Lord in the air. And thus we shall always be with the Lord" (1 Thessalonians 4:16, 17).

- "Behold, I tell you a mystery: We shall not all sleep, but we shall all be changed—in a moment, in the twinkling of an eye, at the last trumpet. For the trumpet will sound, and the dead will be raised incorruptible, and we shall be changed" (1 Corinthians 15:51, 52).

The language used is consistent. The dead are simply dead, awaiting the last day, when the resurrection will take place.

Perhaps one of the most interesting and detailed descriptions of a future resurrection of the dead is found in what some believe to be the oldest book of the Bible. Pay close attention to the sequence of events Job describes:

"But man dies and is laid away; indeed he breathes his last and where is he? As water disappears from the sea, and a river becomes parched and dries up, so man lies down and does not rise. Till the heavens are no more, they will not awake nor be roused from their sleep.

"Oh, that You would hide me in the grave, that You would conceal me until Your wrath is past, that You would appoint me a set time, and remember me! If a man dies, shall he live again? All the days of my hard service I will wait, till my change comes. You shall call, and I will answer You; You shall desire the work of Your hands" (Job 14:10–15).

Job doesn't sound at all like a Greek philosopher on his

way to paradise. He believes that after he dies, he will be hidden in the grave, asleep, until the moment God calls him back to life. Jesus said the same thing: "The hour is coming in which all who are in the graves will hear His voice and come forth" (John 5:28). This will happen when "the heavens are no more," which takes place at the Second Coming (see 2 Peter 3:10; Revelation 6:14).

Job doesn't expect to break free from a physical existence at all. He expects a reboot, a *new* physical existence. Notice the complete absence of ethereal ghosts and spirits in his expectations: "I know that my Redeemer lives, and He shall stand at last on the earth; and after my skin is destroyed, this I know, that *in my flesh* I shall see God" (Job 19:25, 26; emphasis added).

Job expected to live again *in the flesh*. The Bible simply doesn't picture people as becoming ghosts when they die. Never. Whatever it is that Socrates was expecting, the Hebrews didn't know about it. They expected *death*. "The soul who sins shall die," the book of Ezekiel cautions (Ezekiel 18:4, 20). "The wages of sin is death," writes Paul (Romans 6:23). "You must not eat from the tree of the knowledge of good and evil," warned God in Eden, "for when you eat of it you will surely die" (Genesis 2:17).

No continued existence elsewhere. No floating off to philosophers' paradise. Just death.

No wonder Jesus found death so troubling.

Chapter 4

Of Enoch, Moses, and Elijah

We've seen that the Bible says death is just that—*death*. No ongoing, conscious life. No disembodied spirits. No ghosts of dead people. Instead, in the Bible, death is likened to a sleep.

But the ancient Hebrews knew of a handful of people who went to be with God ahead of time. What do their continued lives tell us about death?

Enoch was one of these people. He developed a relationship with God that was so profound that God simply took him straight to heaven without his tasting death. "By faith, Enoch was taken away so that he did not see death, and was not found, because God had taken him" (Hebrews 11:5; cf. Genesis 5:24).

Elijah also went straight to heaven without dying. "Then it happened, as they continued on and talked, that suddenly a chariot of fire appeared with horses of fire, and separated the two of them; and Elijah went up by a whirlwind into heaven" (2 Kings 2:11).

So, there is a grand total of two people who went straight to heaven without dying, and they're clearly exceptions to the rule. The rest of us die and wait for the resurrection. At least, most of us do. There are a few people who died and then enjoyed an early resurrection. They, too, are already in heaven.

The most notable example of an already resurrected person is Moses. He appeared at the Transfiguration on the mount alongside Elijah (Matthew 17, Mark 9, and Luke 9), even though the book of Deuteronomy is quite clear that Moses died and was put to rest in a grave (Deuteronomy 34:5, 6).

How could Moses appear on earth some fifteen hundred years after his death if there are no disembodied spirits?

The answer is simple: he didn't appear as a disembodied spirit. He appeared as who he was—Moses, in the flesh. It takes a bit of detective work, but the mystery can be unraveled from the rest of Scripture. The first thing to notice is that Moses' burial took place under unusual circumstances: "So Moses the servant of the LORD died there in the land of Moab, according to the word of the LORD. And He buried him in a valley in the land of Moab, opposite Beth Peor; but no one knows his grave to this day" (Deuteronomy 34:5, 6).

God Himself buried Moses. Nobody else has known the location of his grave.

Why did God take charge of the interment? Some have suggested that God buried Moses secretly in an unmarked grave to avoid the practices of other Semitic tribes in the area (such as the Canaanites) who were in the habit of worshiping their dead ancestors.

The second thing to notice is that the story of Moses doesn't stop with his burial. An old Hebrew story that isn't in the Bible says God raised him from the dead.* This story, *The Assumption of Moses,* pictures Moses giving his parting instruc-

---

* This story came to light in the mid-nineteenth century when a damaged sixth-century Latin translation of it was found.

tions to Joshua before his "assumption"—his *bodily* reception into heaven. The manuscript describes his death and burial, so we know that it isn't an alternate account of Moses' demise, and we know that it doesn't teach that Moses didn't die. It simply presents his death followed by his "assumption."

The conclusion? Moses was resurrected at some point after his death.

Of course, this story isn't from the Bible. It's just a story. But it does demonstrate what the Jews who lived in the early part of the New Testament era (when the original manuscript is thought to have been written) believed about the fate of Moses.

Ancient writers, such as the early Christian leader Origen, refer to *The Assumption of Moses* when trying to explain an enigmatic passage found in Jude's letter: "Michael the archangel, in contending with the devil, when he disputed about the body of Moses, dared not bring against him a reviling accusation, but said, 'The Lord rebuke you!' " (Jude 9).

Unlike *The Assumption of Moses,* Jude's account of Moses' whereabouts *is* part of the Bible, and the fact that Origen points us to that nonbiblical work when explaining Jude strongly suggests that Jude was in agreement with at least portions of the story. Unfortunately, we only have part of *The Assumption of Moses;* about a third of the work appears to be missing. Some scholars speculate that the account mentioned in Jude may have been a direct quote from the missing part. Others have suggested that Jude pulled the story from a number of ancient sources. Whatever the case, we know that the Jews understood that Moses did *not* remain in his grave, and the book of Jude gives us inspired confirmation that they are right.

The question is *why* the devil would contend with Michael, the archangel, over the body of Moses. If Moses was simply dead, that ought to have satisfied the fallen angel—another sinner had met with his just fate. Lucifer himself was removed from heaven and doomed because of his rebellion, so every other sinner deserves the same fate—case closed.

Unless, of course, *Moses didn't stay in the grave.* At that point, the devil would seem to have a legitimate grievance: How could God overlook the sins of Moses while holding Lucifer accountable for his sins?

A legitimate grievance

Lucifer's grievance *would* be legitimate if it weren't for the provision for sinners that Jesus made at the cross. He died for us "while we were still sinners" (Romans 5:8). He was crucified to "bear the sins of many" (Hebrews 9:28). He was made "to be sin for us, that we might become the righteousness of God in Him" (2 Corinthians 5:21). He gave "His life a ransom for many" (Matthew 20:28). Through His death, Jesus has "redeemed us to God by His blood" (Revelation 5:9). In short, our sin problem has been solved. We have been reconciled to God through the sacrifice of Christ.

But when Moses died, the Crucifixion had not yet taken place. There was no legal justification for taking a sinner into the kingdom of heaven, and the devil would seem to have a reason to dispute what Jesus was doing with the body of Moses, since it was no longer in the grave where it belonged because of Moses' sin. In Luke's account of the Transfiguration, he mentions an interesting detail—the nature of the discussion Moses had with Jesus the day he appeared to the disciples. "And behold, two men talked with Him, who were Moses and Elijah, who appeared in glory and spoke of His decease which He was about to accomplish at Jerusalem" (Luke 9:30, 31).

What was the topic of discussion? The Crucifixion. The solution to the sin problem. Moses and Elijah were already in heaven, and Jesus was about to confirm their right to be there. He was about to make His sacrificial atonement. If Jesus didn't go through with the cross, they wouldn't be allowed to remain alive, never mind to stay in heaven. It's not hard to imagine why Moses and Elijah were so keenly interested in what was about to take place.

Once you set aside the stories we were raised on and begin

to look at what the Bible actually says, some of the more difficult passages begin to make sense. Moses and Elijah weren't
ghosts. They're were—and are—real people. They could make
an appearance at the Transfiguration because they both were
alive physically as well as spiritually: one of them had been
taken straight to heaven in physical form, and the other had
been resurrected—which means he was brought back to life
physically as well as in every other sense. Neither of them was
a ghost.

In fact, the Bible stresses that each of us will have physical, material bodies in the resurrection—just as Jesus had after His resurrection. Notice that Jesus believed this to be
important enough that He demonstrated to His disciples that
it was true. He went out of His way to show that was the case
with Him. He emphasized the difference between His resurrection and what the spiritualistic beliefs of the pagan nations
that surrounded Israel led them to believe resurrection meant.
(Over the course of Israel's history, those beliefs had trickled
into popular Jewish thought.) Jesus showed His disciples that
He wasn't a disembodied spirit or a ghost. He said, "Why are
you troubled? And why do doubts arise in your hearts? Behold My hands and My feet, that it is I Myself. Handle Me
and see, for a spirit does not have flesh and bones as you see I
have" (Luke 24:38, 39).

Jesus was *real,* and He ate fish and honeycomb to prove it
(see Luke 24:41–43). And when *we* come back from the
dead, we will have real, physical bodies like His. "Our citizenship is in heaven, from which we also eagerly wait for the
Savior, the Lord Jesus Christ, who will transform our lowly
body that it may be conformed to His glorious body, according to the working by which He is able even to subdue all
things to Himself" (Philippians 3:20, 21).

See? No ghosts. In fact, the story of the Transfiguration
offers us an important key to understanding how it's going to
work. Just before Matthew gives us his version of the story, he
reports a statement Jesus made that has caused no end of

confusion among modern Christians: "The Son of Man will come in the glory of His Father with His angels, and then He will reward each according to his works. Assuredly, I say to you, there are some standing here who shall not taste death till they see the Son of Man coming in His kingdom" (Matthew 16:27, 28).

Everybody who was there when Jesus spoke those words has been dead for nearly two thousand years. This fact has caused some people to go through unbelievable contortions trying to make sense of this statement. I've heard some people try to explain it by suggesting that it is a last-day prophecy—that the Second Coming will take place while the generation living at the time of the rebirth of Israel (1948) are still alive. Each passing year makes that increasingly less likely, though there's still a little time left. But honestly, to make the passage say that, you have to rip it clear out of its context.

I've heard other people suggest that this story is simply one of the Bible's glaring contradictions; that Jesus believed that He'd be coming back in a few short years, but He got it wrong. He was mistaken.

Still others suggest that Jesus was referring to the destruction of Jerusalem in A.D. 70—an apocalyptic event that *did* take place during the lives of some of those present.

The simplest answer

The simplest answer is usually the right one. That's certainly true here. The seemingly cryptic statement comes at the end of Matthew 16. However, if you want to understand what it means, you can't stop at the end of chapter 16. You have to keep reading a ways into the next chapter.

The original text of the Bible wasn't divided into the chapters and verses we have come to rely on today. They were added long after the Bible was written—in the late Middle Ages and early Reformation periods, in fact—to make it easier to refer to and find passages in the Bible.

Chapters and verses are handy, but they make unnatural

divisions in what the Bible says—as is the case in this story. People tend to stop reading at the end of chapter 16, but Matthew intended for us to keep going.

Jesus' promise that some of the audience would see "the Son of Man coming in His kingdom" is followed immediately by the Transfiguration story. And sure enough, when we consider the Transfiguration carefully, we find that some people—three of the disciples—*did* see Jesus in His glorious kingdom. The Transfiguration was the Second Coming in miniature. In it, we see the glorified Jesus with a person who died and was resurrected and with another person who had been caught up straight into heaven without dying. Compare this with Paul's description of the Second Coming in 1 Thessalonians 4. There he says that at the return of Jesus the righteous dead will rise from their graves to join those who are alive, and together they will meet Jesus.

The story of the Transfiguration fits very neatly with the assertions made in the rest of the Bible that the dead *sleep* until Jesus comes (which is, after all, the expression used by Paul to describe the event). Once we stop reading our twenty-first-century misconceptions into the text, much of what we find confusing starts to make sense. The Bible doesn't present a mishmash of contradictory concepts of death; it presents a unified understanding held by dozens of authors across the span of nearly fifteen hundred years. The only real question is how we have managed to get so far off the track.

The river Styx

I mentioned the answer to this question a little earlier: Israel picked up the traditions and superstitions of surrounding pagan nations. God told them to strictly maintain a distance between themselves and the nations around them so that they wouldn't compromise their beliefs and their covenant relationship with God. In fact, God was so serious about this requirement that He instructed the Israelites to *empty* the land of Canaan of all its occupants.

They didn't do it.

Worse, they began to assimilate the beliefs of their neighbors. That was what resulted in the long, tragic tale of apostate kings that is found in the Old Testament. Even before the Israelites moved to Canaan, they added elements of Egyptian religion, like bovine worship, to their worship. (Remember the golden calf?) When they got to Canaan, some of them worshiped idols in the groves, a practice they learned from the neighboring tribes. And when Ahab married Jezebel, she brought idol worship right into the palace of the king. If people associate with a competing religion intimately enough, it's bound to rub off on them.

The non-Hebrew Semitic tribes had an interesting understanding of the universe. They believed in three realms of existence: the abode of the sky gods (Baal was one of them), the human realm on the surface of the earth, and the realm of the dead in Sheol, a shadowy and poorly understood place that housed some subterranean gods and what was left of humans when they died.

The Greeks were great proponents of this kind of thinking—perhaps the most influential ancient culture to promulgate it. They imagined that a river separated the realm of those who lived on earth from Hades—the underworld, the realm of the shadowy dead. A ferryman by the name of Charon took the deceased across the river into the abode of the dead, where a fierce dog, Cerberus, prevented all who were there from ever leaving. Families would sometimes place a coin on the mouth of a corpse (or *in* the mouth, to prevent theft) in order to pay the ferry toll across the river.

If you were a fan of 1970s music, you'll recognize the name of the river, which a well-known band of that era adopted as their own: Styx.

The Hebrews and Sheol

The Hebrews also referred to the abode of the dead as Sheol, but by that they didn't mean a shadowy underworld.

They were simply referring to the grave. Some modern thinkers have suggested that the Hebrew Sheol was analogous to the Greek Hades or even the subterranean hell portrayed in Dante's *Divine Comedy*. That may have been true for the non-Hebrew Semitic tribes; but given that the suffering Job wished he could go to Sheol (Job 14:13, translated "grave"), it seems highly unlikely that the Hebrews thought of Sheol as a dark place of miserable conscious existence. At least in their early history, the children of Abraham understood Sheol as simply a reference to the grave.

Over time, however, God's people began to adopt some of the beliefs of the neighboring cultures, and they dabbled with the idea that the dead were conscious in Sheol. Some toyed with the pagan notion that they might actually be able to contact the dead. One striking example of this is found in the story of Saul, Israel's first king. After repeatedly rebelling against God, he found himself missing the information he had become accustomed to receiving from prophets such as Samuel. His communication with God was compromised, and Samuel was dead.

Out of desperation, Saul consulted the witch of Endor, a local spiritualist medium. Interestingly, Saul had banned all such practitioners from the nation in obedience to God's command to keep Israel distinct from such people and their beliefs. But when his own relationship with God collapsed, Saul wandered into a spiritualist's home looking for counsel. He was desperate for guidance, because Israel was under attack by the Philistines.

> When Saul saw the army of the Philistines, he was afraid, and his heart trembled greatly. And when Saul inquired of the LORD, the LORD did not answer him, either by dreams or by Urim or by the prophets.
>
> Then Saul said to his servants, "Find me a woman who is a medium, that I may go to her and inquire of her."

And his servants said to him, "In fact, there is a woman who is a medium at En Dor."

So Saul disguised himself and put on other clothes, and he went, and two men with him; and they came to the woman by night. And he said, "Please conduct a séance for me, and bring up for me the one I shall name to you."

Then the woman said to him, "Look, you know what Saul has done, how he has cut off the mediums and the spiritists from the land. Why then do you lay a snare for my life, to cause me to die?"

And Saul swore to her by the LORD, saying, "As the LORD lives, no punishment shall come upon you for this thing."

Then the woman said, "Whom shall I bring up for you?"

And he said, "Bring up Samuel for me."

When the woman saw Samuel, she cried out with a loud voice. And the woman spoke to Saul, saying, "Why have you deceived me? For you are Saul!"

And the king said to her, "Do not be afraid. What did you see?"

And the woman said to Saul, "I saw a spirit ascending out of the earth."

So he said to her, "What is his form?"

And she said, "An old man is coming up, and he is covered with a mantle." And Saul perceived that it was Samuel, and he stooped with his face to the ground and bowed down.

Now Samuel said to Saul, "Why have you disturbed me by bringing me up?"

And Saul answered, "I am deeply distressed; for the Philistines make war against me, and God has departed from me and does not answer me anymore, neither by prophets nor by dreams. Therefore I have called you, that you may reveal to me what I should do."

Then Samuel said: "So why do you ask me, seeing the LORD has departed from you and has become your enemy? And the LORD has done for Himself as He spoke by me. For the LORD has torn the kingdom out of your hand and given it to your neighbor, David. Because you did not obey the voice of the LORD nor execute His fierce wrath upon Amalek, therefore the LORD has done this thing to you this day. Moreover the LORD will also deliver Israel with you into the hand of the Philistines. And tomorrow you and your sons will be with me. The LORD will also deliver the army of Israel into the hand of the Philistines."

Immediately Saul fell full length on the ground, and was dreadfully afraid because of the words of Samuel. And there was no strength in him, for he had eaten no food all day or all night (1 Samuel 28:5–20).

At first glance, this story seems to contradict everything we've discovered about the biblical understanding of death. If the dead are sleeping, unaware of and utterly disconnected from what takes place on earth, how in the world does Samuel suddenly come back from the grave to chat with Saul? Can the dead wake up from their nap to contact the living?

Not at all. The spiritualist medium was *not* a faithful Israelite, if she was an Israelite at all. She was engaged in practices that God had specifically forbidden. In fact, once she discovered that her visitor was Saul, the king who had outlawed her livelihood, she became afraid for her life. She was practicing a forbidden religion; her understanding of the grave was utterly different than that of the Hebrews. She was among those who consider Sheol to be a dark underworld where dead people continue a conscious existence in the shadows.

It's important to pay close attention to the details. If the dead go immediately to the presence of the Lord, why does the woman claim to bring Samuel *up* from the ground? During the séance when Saul asked her what she was seeing, she said, "I saw a spirit ascending out of the earth." Don't miss the fact that *she saw* the spirit and he did not. In the King James Version, this was translated, "I saw *gods* ascending out of the earth." Remember, the Canaanites believed that there were gods of the underworld who ruled over the dead, quite distinct from the gods who ruled the world of the living from the sky.

Whoever this spiritual being at the séance was, he definitely was *not* Samuel. The odds that God would be at the beck and call of a medium, obliged to obey her commands, are nonexistent. Consulting spiritists was an activity He had specifically forbidden. So, whoever this was, it wasn't Samuel. Nor was it the departed spirit of any other human being. If the woman actually saw something, it was far more likely to have been the sort of being that slithered into Eden to declare that sinners would "not surely die" (Genesis 3:4). The fact that the spirit being accepted Saul's worship is particularly telling.

God didn't suddenly lift the veil between the living and the dead at Endor. This is simply a story that shows us an Israelite king dabbling in a non-Israelite religion, and the perilous consequences of doing so: Saul ends up dead. If anything, this story underscores what the Hebrew religion did *not* contain.

Where did it come from?

So how do we explain the majority understanding of the Judeo-Christian religions regarding death—which includes a conscious state of disembodiment?

It's really quite simple: the Hebrews were, over the course of millennia, exposed to pagan cultures—from Egypt to Canaan, and from Babylon to Rome—that held this belief. Some of those cultures quite literally conquered and ruled the children of Israel. The most notable shift in thinking came at the hands of the Greeks, who introduced dualistic philosophy into mainstream Jewish life.

> Unlike the earlier Jewish monotheists, the Hellenistic Jews believed in the immortality of the individual human soul. For those Jews influenced by Greek ideas, at death angels approached and greeted the soul and invited it to mount a chariot which traveled to a far-off place. The body remained behind to be buried a few days later. The virtuous soul lived on the Isles of the Blest of Greek mythology or in the transcendent realms of Plato's eternal ideas. There the soul spent its everlasting days in the company of other souls, angels, and ultimately God. Although the imagery remains vague, we see a heaven of philosophers contemplating abstract ideas and ideal forms without being distracted by other people or the necessities of human life. Scholars might continue their research, which would be easier after the soul's release from the body. The body no longer hampered and distracted the spirit.[1]

The Greeks were profoundly influential. Even their conquerors, the Romans, borrowed heavily from them. In fact, when the Romans rose to power, they continued to use Greek as a language of learning and culture, only replacing it with Latin later on. And even now, much of the way we think as citizens of the Western world was shaped by Greek philosophers.

Under Greek administration, the city of Alexandria (named for Alexander the Great and still the second largest city in Egypt) became a powerful center of learning and the home of the largest library in the world. There was a sizable Jewish community present at the founding of the city, and, as can be expected, they began to enjoy Greek culture and absorb Greek learning. In the earlier stages of their settlement in North Africa, they kept to themselves in one part of the city; later on, under the Romans, they were to be found diffused throughout the community.

Did Alexandrian Jews have their own culture and beliefs, distinct from the Greeks? Of course, but it is difficult to remain immersed in an influential pagan culture for long and not pick up its concepts and attitudes. Immigrant communities provide vivid examples of how quickly this can happen. My father is a Dutch immigrant to Canada. I grew up in a virtual ghetto of Dutch immigrants; but I was educated outside of that tight-knit community, and I didn't marry a Dutch girl. Today, culturally, I am more North American than Dutch. Immigrants of every stripe invariably face this challenge when they immerse their children in a new culture. Egyptian Jews not were excepted.

What the Egyptian Jews could not accept

There were aspects of Greek belief, of course, that Egyptian Jews could *not* accept. As the most notable monotheistic religion in history to that point, they wouldn't adopt the pantheon of Greek gods or many of the pagan practices that went with the veneration of those gods. They rejected Greek religion, but they adored Greek philosophy—so much so that some argued that the Greeks must have originally gotten their brilliant ideas from the Jews and then corrupted them with paganism.

> The Greek-speaking Jews of Alexandria were familiar with the works of the ancient Greek poets and philosophers and acknowledged their universal appeal. They would not, however, give up their own religion, nor could they accept the prevailing Hellenistic culture with its polytheistic foundations and pagan practice. Thus they came to create their own version of Hellenistic culture. They contended that

Greek philosophy had derived its concepts from Jewish sources and that there was no contradiction between the two systems of thought. On the other hand, they also gave Judaism an interpretation of their own, turning the Jewish concept of God into an abstraction and His relationship to the world into a subject of metaphysical speculation. Alexandrine Jewish philosophers stressed the universal aspects of Jewish law and the prophets, de-emphasized the national Jewish aspects of Jewish religion, and sought to provide rational motives for Jewish religious practice. In this manner they sought not only to defend themselves against the onslaught of the prevailing pagan culture, but also to spread monotheism and respect for the high moral and ethical values of Judaism. The basis of Jewish-Hellenistic literature was the Septuagint, the Greek translation of the Bible, which was to become the cornerstone of a new world culture. . . . The apologetic tendency of Jewish-Hellenistic culture is clearly discernible in the Septuagint. Alexandrine Jewish literature sought to express the concepts of the Jewish-Hellenistic culture and to propagate these concepts among Jews and Gentiles. Among these Jewish writers there were poets, playwrights, and historians; but it was the philosophers who made a lasting contribution. Philo of Alexandria was the greatest among them, but also the last of any significance.[2]

Between Greek domination in the Middle East and Alexandrian educational influence, the shadowy ideas of a conscious afterlife made their way into mainstream Jewish culture. Alexandria later became a center for Christian learning as well, producing such early luminaries as Origen, who was known as a master of Greek philosophy and as the author of his own neo-Platonic work, *On First Principles*. While by no means the only early Christian to dabble in dualistic thinking, Origen is a prime example of Alexandrian influence on the Judeo-Christian tradition. Like his Jewish predecessors, he was opposed to Greek religion but not to Greek philosophy:

> After these points, also, the apostolic teaching is that the soul, having a substance and life of its own, shall, after its departure from the world, be rewarded according to its deserts, being destined to obtain either an inheritance of eternal life and blessedness, if its actions shall have procured this for it, or to be delivered up to eternal fire and punishments, if the guilt of its crimes shall have brought it down to this: and also, that there is to be a time of resurrection from the dead, when this body, which now "is sown in corruption, shall rise in incorruption," and that which "is sown in dishonour will rise in glory."[3]

One of Origen's more controversial ideas—one that failed to find acceptance among Christians—was the idea that souls actually existed *before* they were implanted in human bodies. Origen suggested that two creation events are recorded in the book of Genesis, the first of which was the creation of souls without bodies. Given free will, these spirits fell from grace, and some of them became corporeal human beings.

Of course, this interpretation of the story of the Creation and the Fall didn't make it into mainstream Christianity because it was simply too far outside the pale of orthodoxy. More acceptable was Origen's insistence that the soul continues to survive after death. The Jews of Alexandria, and by extension the Christians of that city, had been steeped in Greek philosophy long enough to find that notion perfectly palatable.

As Origen defended the idea of preexistent and posthumous human souls, he leaned on Plato's philosophy as much (or more) than he did on the Bible. In his attempts to align the Bible with Greek philosophy, he claimed the stories in the Bible were to be understood as being allegories rather than literal history. And to make the worlds of Hebrew and Greek thought compatible, he performed great feats of *eisegesis*— twisting Scripture to fit his own interpretation of it. Even though he is honored as a leader of the early Christian church, the honor given him is somewhat limited because of his Gnostic and Platonic leanings and his allegorical interpretation of Scripture. Today, some Christians consider him an outright heretic. Origen's ideas on death, however, were in keeping with the new ideas that were popular in Alexandria before his time, and they found easy acceptance.

Notice in the above quotation Origen's declaration that "the apostolic teaching is that the soul, having a substance and life of its own, shall, after its departure from the world, be rewarded according to its deserts." In other words, nearly two centuries after most of the apostles had died, and well over a century after the last of them died, Origen told his readers that Christ's disciples believed the notion that the human soul breaks free of its material prison at death and goes on to its reward—either in heaven or hell.

He was taking people on a journey across the Styx. He was quoting Plato, not the apostles, for they believed no such thing.

Endnotes

1. Colleen McDannell and Bernhard Lang, *Heaven: A History* (New Haven, CT: Yale University Press, 1988), 18.

2. "Alexandria," Jewish Virtual Library, accessed June 20, 2014, http://www.jewishvirtuallibrary.org/jsource/judaica/ejud_0002_0001 _0_00765.html.

3. A. Cleveland Coxe, preface to *De Principiis,* by Origen, quoted in Philip Schaff, ed., *Ante-Nicene Fathers* (Grand Rapids: Eerdmans, 1885), 4:239, http://www.ccel.org/ccel/schaff/anf04.vi.v.i.html.

Interlude

Two Stories Jesus Told

When I first started to examine the Bible's passages on death and realized that it taught an unconscious sleep rather than a disembodied existence, a couple of important questions occurred to me. There was no doubt that the death-as-sleep motif was pervasive throughout the New Testament, and it was clear that the authors of the New Testament spoke of no other possibility. However, two passages in the Bible didn't seem to fit this perspective: the story of the thief on the cross, and the story of the rich man and Lazarus. Both of these stories seem to contradict the notion that those who are in Christ but die before the Second Coming simply rest in their graves until that great event takes place.

In the story of the thief, Jesus appears to promise the thief entrance into heaven that very day. And Jesus' story of the rich man and Lazarus seems to suggest that the dead continue to have a conscious existence after they die. That is, they seem to suggest this unless you read them carefully and place them in the context of the rest of Scripture. Let's tackle them one at a time, beginning with the thief on the cross.

There were also two others, criminals, led with Him to be put to death. And when they had come to the place called Calvary, there they crucified Him, and the criminals, one on the right hand and the other on the left. . . . Then one of the criminals who were hanged blasphemed Him, saying, "If You are the Christ, save Yourself and us." But the other, answering, rebuked him, saying, "Do you not even fear God, seeing you are under the same condemnation? And we indeed justly, for we receive the due reward of our deeds; but this Man has done nothing wrong." Then he said to Jesus, "Lord, remember me when You come into Your kingdom." And Jesus said to him, "Assuredly, I say to you, today you will be with Me in Paradise" (Luke 23:32, 33, 39–43).

Confusing, isn't it? It seems to fly in the face of everything else we've examined. The thief is promised that he will arrive in the courts of heaven that very day. Given the fact that Enoch, Moses, and Elijah *were* taken to heaven, that's not out of the realm of possibility. God either could rescue the thief from the cross and assume him bodily into heaven, or He could raise him from the dead later that afternoon. But that isn't the sense in which most Christians read this story: they believe that his *ghost* was about to go to heaven.

That view of death raises three key problems.

1. *The thief didn't die that day.* Crucifixion was an ag-
   onizingly slow way to die—that was why the authorities used it. Most victims suffered for *days*.*
   According to some historians, the Jews didn't
   want ghastly crosses silhouetted against the sky

---

* That speaks volumes about the death of Christ. The fact that He died in a matter of hours tells us that it wasn't just the nails that killed Him; the weight of our sins was also crushing Him.

during the Sabbath hours, so the crosses were laid on the ground as sunset approached on Friday. This posed a problem in that some victims were strong enough to escape.

The Bible tells us how the Romans solved this problem. As the end of Friday drew near, they broke the legs of those who were still alive. Notice that this is what John reports happened to the thief (John 19:32, 33). This, of course, had the added effect of hastening death in the coming days—but it also informs us that the thief did *not* die on the day when Jesus made His promise to the thief, which, of course, means he didn't go to heaven on that day.

2. *Jesus didn't go to heaven that day either.* In keeping with the biblical understanding that the dead are asleep, Jesus was simply resting *in the grave* during the hours between His death and His resurrection. It's important to notice what Jesus said shortly *after* the resurrection when He appeared to Mary and she tried to touch him. His words? "Do not cling to Me, for I have not yet ascended to My Father; but go to My brethren and say to them, 'I am ascending to My Father and your Father, and to My God and your God' " (John 20:17). Jesus said He was *going* to ascend to heaven, and, more tellingly, He said He had not been there yet. Obviously, if Jesus hadn't gone to heaven during the time between His death and resurrection, the thief couldn't have been there with Him the day of the crucifixion.

3. *Jesus' kingdom was not established that day.* The thief asked to be remembered when Jesus came into His kingdom. Matthew's Gospel pictures Jesus as saying that He'll be enthroned when He comes back to this world in glory: "When the Son of Man comes in His glory, and all the holy angels

with Him, then He will sit on the throne of His glory" (Matthew 25:31). Likewise, the remarkable prophecy of Daniel 2 shows us—through the vivid imagery of a stone that fills the earth after destroying a statue—that God establishes His kingdom after all of the world's other kingdoms have been destroyed. And Daniel 7 shows us Jesus receiving His everlasting kingdom after the judgment has concluded.

Given the context of the rest of the Bible, Jesus' words to the thief cannot *possibly* mean that he would join Jesus in the kingdom that very day.

So, did Jesus make a mistake? Not likely. It's important to remember that the New Testament was written without chapter and verse numbers, as I've already pointed out. It was also written without punctuation, which can prove to be a challenge for translators. When the Bible was translated into English during the fifteenth and sixteenth centuries, the translators placed punctuation marks wherever they thought they should be.

Of course, sometimes they placed it in accordance with their own understanding—consequently, our English Bibles have Jesus saying, "Assuredly, I say to you, today you will be with Me in Paradise." Punctuated this way, Jesus' promise to the thief says he'll be in heaven that very day—the day on which he made the request.

But simply remove the comma after the word *you,* or better yet, remove it from there and place it after the word *today,* and it suddenly makes more sense: "Assuredly, I say to you today, you will be with Me in Paradise."*

Make that change and this little story fits the rest of

---

* It's remarkable what a difference a comma can make. Perhaps you've seen the meme circulating on the Internet that powerfully illustrates the difference between "Let's eat, Grandma!" and "Let's eat Grandma!"

Scripture. The thief is not going to heaven that day; he is being given a guarantee that day. Jesus is reassuring him that afternoon that he can count on it—he *will* be with Jesus in Paradise. In effect, Jesus is saying, "I'm telling you right now, as we hang on these crosses, as the rest of the world mocks us, as the situation seems utterly hopeless, that you can rest in the knowledge that you will be with Me when I come into My kingdom."

Remove or correct the punctuation added centuries later, and the apparent contradiction simply disappears. This story, as is true of every other story in the Bible, exists in complete agreement with the rest of the book.

The rich man and Lazarus

The other apparent difficulty is found in the story of the rich man and Lazarus—or more precisely, the *parable* of the rich man and Lazarus. It's important to note that this is not a factual account but a story Jesus tells to illustrate a point. It occurs in a series of parables, each one of which begins with the telltale phrase "a certain man."

- The parable of the rich fool begins in Luke 12:16: "The ground of a certain rich man yielded plentifully."
- The parable of the vineyard begins in Luke 13:6: "A certain man had a fig tree planted in his vineyard."
- The parable of the supper feast begins in Luke 14:16: "A certain man gave a great supper and invited many."
- The parable of the prodigal son begins in Luke 15:11: "A certain man had two sons."
- The parable of the unfaithful steward begins in Luke 16:1: "There was a certain rich man who had a steward."

So the parallel between the beginning of the story of the rich man and Lazarus and the beginnings of these other stories that are parables identifies it also as being a parable. Notice how similar to the other parables this story is.

"There was a certain rich man who was clothed in purple and fine linen and fared sumptuously every day. But there was a certain beggar named Lazarus, full of sores, who was laid at his gate, desiring to be fed with the crumbs which fell from the rich man's table. Moreover the dogs came and licked his sores. So it was that the beggar died, and was carried by the angels to Abraham's bosom. The rich man also died and was buried. And being in torments in Hades, he lifted up his eyes and saw Abraham afar off, and Lazarus in his bosom.

"Then he cried and said, 'Father Abraham, have mercy on me, and send Lazarus that he may dip the tip of his finger in water and cool my tongue; for I am tormented in this flame.' But Abraham said, 'Son, remember that in your lifetime you received your good things, and likewise Lazarus evil things; but now he is comforted and you are tormented. And besides all this, between us and you there is a great gulf fixed, so that those who want to pass from here to you cannot, nor can those from there pass to us.'

"Then he said, 'I beg you therefore, father, that you would send him to my father's house, for I have five brothers, that he may testify to them, lest they also come to this place of torment.' Abraham said to him, 'They have Moses and the prophets; let them hear them.' And he said, 'No, father Abraham; but if one goes to them from the dead, they will repent.' But he said to him, 'If they do not hear Moses and the prophets, neither will they be persuaded though one rise from the dead' " (Luke 16:19–31).

It's important to note that the language used in this story is clearly symbolic; it cannot be a literal account. If it *were* a literal account, it would be immediately problematic:*

- The dead are said to be living in Abraham's "bosom," or chest.
- The dead in hell would be able to watch and communicate with the dead in heaven and vice versa. It is hard to imagine a paradise where the saved can witness the perpetual suffering of the wicked.
- The language used and actions contemplated (e.g., dipping fingers in water to cool tongues) don't fit the characters if they are disembodied ghosts.

It is important to remember that thanks to the influence of Greek rule and of its schools at Alexandria, some sects of Jews had already dabbled in Greek dualism. The Pharisees were apparently among those who had bought into the possibility that the dead were somehow conscious after death. (This comes up in Paul's dispute with them in Acts 23:6–9.)

The context in which Jesus tells this parable has nothing to do with the state of human beings in death. Instead, it comes on the heels of a discourse about their self-righteous attitude and their assumption of superiority. Jesus is driving home the important point that they are further from the kingdom than are the Gentiles whom they scorn, and He is using a story they would relate to (and possibly would themselves have told in some varied form) to illustrate something altogether unrelated to the subject of death. Jesus was not endorsing their position on the nature of death. He was using their own thinking—one of their own stories—to illustrate a different subject. Notice some of the key details:

- The rich man is described as royalty: dressed in purple and fine linen.

---

* It is something other than literal only in the fact that the rest of the Bible, including Jesus' earlier statements in John 11, says death is like an unconscious sleep.

- He has plenty to eat; he's faring sumptuously.
- The rich man refers to Abraham as "father."
- The family of the rich man has "Moses and the prophets."
- Lazarus is a beggar who sits outside at the gate with the dogs, hoping to glean a few crumbs that fall to the floor.

The Pharisees would have immediately grasped what Jesus was saying; they often referred to Gentiles as unclean dogs. On another occasion, a Canaanite woman approached Jesus asking for help, and to illustrate the attitude of many Israelites, Jesus says to her, "It is not good to take the children's bread and throw it to the little dogs" (Matthew 15:26). Of course, the rest of Jesus' ministry demonstrates conclusively that He didn't actually feel that way Himself.

The nation of Israel was told to be a "light to the Gentiles," to share their blessings and bring the rest of the world into the family of God. (See, e.g., Isaiah 42:6; 49:6; 60:3; Acts 13:47.) Instead, they went in one and then the other of two possible directions. Prior to the Babylonian captivity, they allowed the Gentiles to become a light to *them,* and they abandoned their own faith. Upon returning from captivity, they became so paranoid of compromise that they isolated themselves from the Gentiles, whom they considered to be unclean dogs.

It is entirely possible that Jesus had this Canaanite woman in mind when He told the story of the rich man and Lazarus. At any rate, His audience would have understood quite clearly who was sitting by the gate with the dogs: the Gentiles. In this parable, they are pictured as hungry, hoping for the gospel, waiting for the spiritually rich Hebrews to share what they know.

Jesus is addressing the Pharisees through the character of the rich man, because, like him, they assumed that they were naturally part of God's kingdom and were highly favored by Him. They expected that when David's throne was reestablished, they would play a very important role in the new order.

But in Jesus' story, the tables are suddenly turned: the rich man loses everything, and Lazarus joins the family of Abraham. Paul reaffirms this understanding quite beautifully when he later tells the Galatians, "If you are Christ's, then you are Abraham's seed, and heirs according to the promise" (Galatians 3:29).

One of the saddest themes in the New Testament is the looming consequences for the Jews' persistent rebellion. "He came to His own," John tells us, "and His own did not receive Him" (John 1:11). As Daniel was examining a prophecy by Jeremiah that the Babylonian captivity would end after seventy years, the angel Gabriel reveals that Israel's second chance wouldn't last forever: "Seventy weeks are determined for your people and for your holy city, to finish the transgression, to make an end of sins, to make reconciliation for iniquity, to bring in everlasting righteousness, to seal up vision and prophecy, and to anoint the Most Holy" (Daniel 9:24).

The prophecy ends a few verses later with a second devastation of Israel, which of course happened when the Roman general Titus sacked the city and destroyed the temple in A.D. 70. Gabriel was letting Daniel know that there was a defined period of time set aside for Israel, during which time they would be on probation. It was seventy prophetic weeks, which translates to a literal period of 490 years.* The pending close of that probationary period is an ever-present theme in the ministry of Jesus:

---

* Days are often used to represent years in Bible prophecy; see Numbers 14:34 and Ezekiel 4:6 for vivid examples. The seventy prophetic weeks are made up of 490 prophetic days, which represent 490 literal years. This is why Bible scholars assign a much longer period than seventy literal weeks to this prophecy, a practice that is confirmed by its stunning accuracy in predicting key events in Jesus' life, such as His baptism and crucifixion. See my book *The Appearing* for a detailed exposition.

- "And do not think to say to yourselves, 'We have Abraham as our father.' For I say to you that God is able to raise up children to Abraham from these stones. And even now the ax is laid to the root of the trees. Therefore every tree which does not bear good fruit is cut down and thrown into the fire" (Matthew 3:9, 10).
- "But when the king heard about it, he was furious. And he sent out his armies, destroyed those murderers, and burned up their city" (Matthew 22:7).*
- "O Jerusalem, Jerusalem, the one who kills the prophets and stones those who are sent to her! How often I wanted to gather your children together, as a hen gathers her chicks under her wings, but you were not willing! See! Your house is left to you desolate" (Matthew 23:37, 38).

Later on, Paul and Barnabas underscored the eventual fulfillment of this prediction in terms that reflect the themes of the parable of Lazarus.

> Then Paul and Barnabas grew bold and said, "It was necessary that the word of God should be spoken to you first; but since you reject it, and judge yourselves unworthy of everlasting life, behold, we turn to the Gentiles. For so the Lord has commanded us:
>
> > " 'I have set you as a light to the Gentiles, that you should be for salvation to the ends of the earth.' "
>
> Now when the Gentiles heard this, they were

---

* Jesus speaks these words at the close of His parable of the marriage supper. After repeated appeals, the invitees actually *killed* the messengers—a reference to the way God's prophets had been treated over the centuries. As a result, the king allows their city to be destroyed.

glad and glorified the word of the Lord. And as many as had been appointed to eternal life believed (Acts 13:46–48).

When the story of the rich man and Lazarus is read within the context of the rest of the New Testament, it becomes abundantly clear that it is not a statement on the afterlife, but is rather a cleverly constructed cautionary parable to warn the proud Pharisees of their impending fate. The beggar who sat with the dogs would find himself in the family of Abraham, and the proud Pharisees would find themselves removed from their place of privilege.

The story ends with a devastating critique of the Pharisees:

> "Then he said, 'I beg you therefore, father, that you would send him to my father's house, for I have five brothers, that he may testify to them, lest they also come to this place of torment.' Abraham said to him, 'They have Moses and the prophets; let them hear them.' And he said, 'No, father Abraham; but if one goes to them from the dead, they will repent.' But he said to him, 'If they do not hear Moses and the prophets, neither will they be persuaded though one rise from the dead' " (Luke 16:27–31).

Remember, Jesus tells this story in the *sixteenth* chapter of Luke. In the *eleventh* chapter of John, He literally raised a man named Lazarus from the dead—a miracle that His critics rejected rather than become believers.

The lesson? If the Bible isn't enough to convince you, a miracle won't do it either, because a calloused heart is a very hard thing to change. People can so deafen themselves to the voice of the Holy Spirit that *nothing* will reach them.

Chapter 5

Life After Death

The early months of the New Testament church were fraught with turmoil, not the least of which was caused by what Peter was preaching in his first public sermons. He was quite blunt in assigning blame for the Crucifixion to his audience: "You killed the long-awaited Messiah" was a common theme. Naturally, this upset the religious authorities, who were hoping that Jesus' execution would be the last of their troubles with Him. Now His disciples were telling people that Jesus was, in fact, not dead.

> "Men of Israel, hear these words: Jesus of Nazareth, a Man attested by God to you by miracles, wonders, and signs which God did through Him in your midst, as you yourselves also know—Him, being delivered by the determined purpose and foreknowledge of God, you have taken by lawless hands, have crucified, and put to death; whom God raised up, having loosed the pains of death, because it was not possible that He should be held by it" (Acts 2:22–24).

"But you denied the Holy One and the Just, and asked for a murderer to be granted to you, and killed the Prince of life, whom God raised from the dead, of which we are witnesses" (Acts 3:14, 15).

Then Peter, filled with the Holy Spirit, said to them, "Rulers of the people and elders of Israel: if we this day are judged for a good deed done to a helpless man, by what means he has been made well, let it be known to you all, and to all the people of Israel, that by the name of Jesus Christ of Nazareth, whom you crucified, whom God raised from the dead, by Him this man stands here before you whole" (Acts 4:8–10).

The sermon from which that last quotation was taken came on the heels of a miraculous healing. A man who had been lame from birth was made whole, and the authorities knew they couldn't deny that something supernatural had happened. "Seeing the man who had been healed standing with them, they could say nothing against it" (verse 14).

Peter's assertion that the power that had healed the man was the same power that Jesus had must have made the authorities feel sick to their stomachs. It was proof that Jesus wasn't dead; now even those who hadn't seen Him since the Resurrection had evidence that He was alive. The high priest Caiaphas must have panicked; after all, Jesus had promised that he (Caiaphas) would one day see Jesus coming in the clouds of glory.

Peter was not only preaching that the dead come back to life; he was *proving* it. The healed man was further evidence that God was able to turn back the tide, to correct the ravages that sin had made on the human race. And if Jesus came back from the dead, everyone else could too.

That was, in fact, the message the apostles delivered to their audiences. You will search in vain for a sermon that presents the dead as disembodied spirits enjoying the presence of God in an ethereal realm. The apostles spoke of a *physical* Jesus who had returned to heaven, which, of course, means that heaven must have a physical location.

Take a look at the story of Acts 4 more closely, and you'll find something interesting. "Now as they spoke to the people, the priests, the captain of the temple, and the Sadducees came upon them, being greatly disturbed that they taught the people and preached in Jesus the resurrection from the dead" (verses 1, 2).

You'll find no mention of ghosts; no mention of a shadowy existence after death. The message was simple: Jesus rose from the dead, and you can too. It's always resurrection that the apostles preach, not transmigration of spirits or ascension to a disembodied realm of existence. The Sadducees struggled with that concept because the members of their sect didn't believe in *any* form of afterlife, not even a physical resurrection from the dead. Apparently, this was a source of contention between the Pharisees and the Sadducees. Later, Paul played upon this dispute to his advantage: "When Paul perceived that one part were Sadducees and the other Pharisees, he cried out in the council, 'Men and brethren, I am a Pharisee, the son of a Pharisee; concerning the hope and resurrection of the dead I am being judged!' " (Acts 23:6).

That was clever! Paul was on trial for his preaching, and he noticed that some of the members of the council were Sadducees, who believed there was no afterlife, and that other members of the council were Pharisees, who believed in the resurrection of the dead and, according to the author Luke, in a spiritual realm. (It's important to note that Luke attributes the more ethereal beliefs, not to Paul, but to the Pharisees, who had been influenced to some extent by foreign ideas.) Paul's message was elegantly simple: we find hope in the resurrection of the dead. Again, we find that the apostles were not telling ghost stories.

In Athens, the center of learning

In the city of Athens, that great center of Greek learning, Paul preached the same simple message: the dead can come back to life: "Then certain Epicurean and Stoic philosophers encountered him [Paul]. And some said, 'What does this babbler want to say?' Others said, 'He seems to be a proclaimer of foreign gods,' because he preached to them Jesus and the resurrection" (Acts 17:18).

The Epicureans and Stoics probably wouldn't have had a problem with Paul telling stories of the underworld; they were used to such ideas. But Paul's message was radical: Jesus came back to life, and we have the hope of the resurrection. And that, in fact, is what Paul expounds upon so eloquently for the church in Corinth in his first letter to them. The passage is important enough to warrant reproducing it at length. Read through it carefully and look for *any* hint of departed ghosts or shadowy underworlds.

> If Christ is preached that He has been raised from the dead, how do some among you say that there is no resurrection of the dead? But if there is no resurrection of the dead, then Christ is not risen. And if Christ is not risen, then our preaching is empty and your faith is also empty. Yes, and we are found false witnesses of God, because we have testified of God that He raised up Christ, whom He did not raise up—if in fact the dead do not rise. For if the dead do not rise, then Christ is not risen. And if Christ is not risen, your faith is futile; you are still in your sins! Then also those who have fallen asleep in Christ have perished. If in this life only we have hope in Christ, we are of all men the most pitiable. But now Christ is risen from the dead, and has become the firstfruits of those who have fallen asleep. For since by man came death, by Man also came the resurrection of the dead. For as in Adam all die,

even so in Christ all shall be made alive. But each one in his own order: Christ the firstfruits, afterward those who are Christ's at His coming. Then comes the end, when He delivers the kingdom to God the Father, when He puts an end to all rule and all authority and power. For He must reign till He has put all enemies under His feet. The last enemy that will be destroyed is death (1 Corinthians 15:12–26).

So far, the message is consistent with everything else we've looked at. The dead are asleep, and if Jesus did not rise from the dead, there is no hope. Paul is putting all of his hopes in a resurrection, not some unquantifiable, disembodied future. He points out that Jesus is only the *first* to rise from the dead; the rest of us will follow His example at the Second Coming.*

This does become confusing in a statement that Paul makes a little later on: "Now this I say, brethren, that flesh and blood cannot inherit the kingdom of God, nor does corruption inherit incorruption" (verse 50).

This line seems to suggest that heaven is a ghostly realm where "flesh and blood" do not exist. But that's not quite what Paul was saying. In this passage, he was comparing the sinful Adam to the sinless Christ. He reminds his readers that death came to the human race through Adam, but life comes

---

* You will note, of course, that Lazarus and a few others were raised from the dead before Jesus' resurrection, chronologically speaking. Paul is comparing Jesus' resurrection to the Feast of Firstfruits, in which Israel took the first ripened grain as a token that God would bless and the rest of the harvest would surely follow. Jesus was first—not chronologically first, but first in importance. It is because He rose that we will rise. This is not unlike referring to someone as the "first officer" or the "First Lady." These terms do not suggest that the people holding these positions are the very first to hold them but that the positions they hold give them preeminence.

through Jesus, who is considered a "second" Adam (see verse 22). The apostles had no doubt that Jesus rose from the grave in a physical body, and Paul doubtless knew the story of how Jesus encouraged Thomas to touch Him in order to dispel any notion that He was anything but physically risen from the dead. When Paul says that flesh and blood do not inherit the kingdom of God, he is referring to Adam's sinful body—the same corrupt body we all have that is subject to death. Jesus' risen body—still a *physical* body—is incorruptible and suitable for life in the kingdom. In fact, Paul contrasts two kinds of flesh. "All flesh is not the same flesh, but there is one kind of flesh of men, another flesh of animals, another of fish, and another of birds. . . . So also is the resurrection of the dead. The body is sown in corruption, it is raised in incorruption" (verses 39, 42).

Both states of being involve a body. The sinful body dies because it is corruptible, but it is raised in an incorruptible state, no longer subject to death. In fact, Paul elsewhere states that we are raised with the same kind of glorified body that Jesus had when He rose from the dead. "Our citizenship is in heaven, from which we also eagerly wait for the Savior, the Lord Jesus Christ, who will transform our lowly body that it may be conformed to His glorious body, according to the working by which He is able even to subdue all things to Himself" (Philippians 3:20, 21).

God's ultimate plan is to restore us to what the human beings who lived in Eden were. He will reverse the effects of sin and lift the curse that we brought on ourselves. And you'll note that Adam and Eve were not created as ghosts but as real, live people who lived in a real, physical place.

Paul ends his thoughts to the Corinthians with one of the most famous of his passages, one that is read at countless Christian funerals. Tragically, its full impact and meaning are often tempered by our modern murky understanding of death.

Behold, I tell you a mystery: We shall not all sleep, but we shall all be changed—in a moment, in the twinkling of an eye, at the last trumpet. For the trumpet will sound, and the dead will be raised incorruptible, and we shall be changed. For this corruptible must put on incorruption, and this mortal must put on immortality. So when this corruptible has put on incorruption, and this mortal has put on immortality, then shall be brought to pass the saying that is written: "Death is swallowed up in victory."

"O Death, where is your sting? O Hades, where is your victory?" (1 Corinthians 15:51–55).

The Bible presents God's plan for His people in unmistakable language. First, we sleep. Then, when Christ returns, at the last trumpet, death is turned on its head and we are raised from the dead. The sleep of those who died in Christ has ended. We are changed; utterly reversing sin's ravages of our bodies. Mortal human beings become immortal human beings.

Personally, I am glad of it. The slow decay our bodies experience in this life will not last forever. The problems of aging are not a permanent state of affairs. Jesus not only provides the opportunity for forgiveness; He utterly and completely undoes all the damage we've suffered because of our rebellion against God. We are forgiven *and ultimately restored.*

Nowhere in all of this will you find mention of ghosts. They're simply not a part of the message the apostles were preaching.

"Present with the Lord"?

But wait a minute, you may be thinking, *doesn't Paul say that to be "absent from the body" is to be "present with the Lord"?*

Yes, he does, sort of. The passage is found in his second letter to the Corinthians. Remember, his assertion that the dead sleep until the resurrection is found in his *first* letter to the Corinthians. Would he teach something completely different in his next letter? Not likely.

Here's what he said in the second letter: "We are confident, yes, well pleased rather to be absent from the body and to be present with the Lord" (2 Corinthians 5:8).

If you read it with the mind of a twenty-first-century Christian, it's easy to assume that Paul was saying that we are whisked into God's presence the moment we die. We become absent from the body, he says, and then we live in heaven *without* a body.

Except that's *not* what Paul was saying. You have to read the passage out of context to make it say that. Elsewhere, Paul was quite definitive about when he expected to receive his heavenly reward. Shortly before his death, he wrote these words to Timothy:

> I am already being poured out as a drink offering, and the time of my departure is at hand. I have fought the good fight, I have finished the race, I have kept the faith. Finally, there is laid up for me the crown of righteousness, which the Lord, the righteous Judge, will give to me on that Day, and not to me only but also to all who have loved His appearing (2 Timothy 4:6–8).

Notice when Paul expects the rewards to be doled out: at the Second Coming. This is not the case for him alone but for "all who have loved His appearing." Everybody gets rewarded at the same moment, a fact that is vividly underlined by the author of the letter to the Hebrews. After listing all of the great heroes of the faith, the author ends the famous "faith chapter" by stating, "All these, having obtained a good testimony through faith, did not receive the promise, God having provided something better for us, that they should not be made perfect apart from us" (Hebrews 11:39, 40).

The book of Revelation ends on the same note:

> "He who is unjust, let him be unjust still; he who is filthy, let him be filthy still; he who is righteous, let him be righteous still; he who is holy, let him be holy still. And behold, I am coming quickly, and My reward is with Me, to give to every one according to his work. I am the Alpha and the Omega, the Beginning and the End, the First and the Last" (Revelation 22:11–13).

The testimony of the New Testament is remarkably consistent: the dead are asleep; they are raised from that sleep when Jesus comes; and the righteous are rewarded at that time. Paul's apparent assertion that we are "present with the Lord" the moment we are "absent from the body" is the only anomaly in the picture the New Testament presents. And when you read this statement of Paul in the context of the rest of the New Testament and in the context of the verse that immediately precedes it, it lines up with every other passage.

> We know that if our earthly house, this tent, is destroyed, we have a building from God, a house not made with hands, eternal in the heavens. For in this we groan, earnestly desiring to be clothed with our habitation which is from heaven, if indeed, having been clothed, we shall not be found naked. For we who are in this tent groan, being burdened, not because we want to be unclothed, but further clothed, that mortality may be swallowed up by life. Now He who has prepared us for this very thing is God, who also has given us the Spirit as a guarantee.
>
> So we are always confident, knowing that while we are at home in the body we are absent from the Lord. For we walk by faith, not by sight. We are

confident, yes, well pleased rather to be absent from the body and to be present with the Lord. Therefore we make it our aim, whether present or absent, to be well pleasing to Him. For we must all appear before the judgment seat of Christ, that each one may receive the things done in the body, according to what he has done, whether good or bad (2 Corinthians 5:1–10).

Remember that in Paul's first letter to this audience, he distinguished the sinless, glorified, "incorruptible" body of Christ from the sinful, "corruptible" body of Adam. He is, in essence, doing the same thing here. In fact, if you read the above passage carefully, you'll notice that he describes three states of being.

1. *The earthly house.* This is a description of the body we presently have, which is subject to sickness, disease, and death. It's like a tent that will be destroyed. We groan and are burdened in this body, hoping for the body we will have in the resurrection.
2. *The building from God.* This is our resurrection body, the incorruptible one we receive when we rise from the dead. It is the "habitation from heaven," a "house not made with hands," "eternal in the heavens." Nowhere does Paul state that it represents an ethereal, disembodied existence. On the contrary, he describes our donning it as being "further clothed." To use his own analogy, he is talking about exchanging tents, not living without one. Our earthly body is replaced by a heavenly body.
3. *Naked, or unclothed.* This is the part that gets modern audiences confused. Because of the presuppositions we bring to the passage, we assume

this means a ghostly, disembodied existence. But to make this passage say that, we would have to lift it away from the rest of Paul's letters and from the rest of the Bible. This nakedness simply pictures the time when those who die in Christ are in the grave; when they're between the two bodies. At that time they have no body. They have no existence. They are between this life and the next and have *nothing*. They are dead, asleep.

It's important to note that Paul doesn't say that they are conscious of anything in this state. They don't have an existence apart from this world or the next. Paul doesn't want to be in this state, which tells us that there must be some point after death when people are *not* in the presence of God.

When Paul concludes his line of reasoning by saying that he wants to be "absent from the body and present with the Lord," he's saying nothing more than that he wishes to be rid of this painful, sin-sick, corruptible body and to begin his life in the next world, the one that follows Jesus' second coming, where he will be in God's presence. I feel exactly the same way. Let eternity begin!

You'll notice that this passage has no time line indicating when this might happen, so we have to read the rest of Paul's writings to find the answer. And Paul says it happens when Jesus comes. At some point—at death—we are done with this corruptible body. At some point—at Jesus' second coming—we begin our existence in God's presence with a new, incorruptible body. There is nothing in this passage that disagrees with the rest of Paul's writings on the subject. The Bible is remarkably consistent.

I've heard some people suggest that when Jesus returns, He brings with Him from heaven the disembodied spirits of the dead. Then He raises their dead bodies and reinserts these souls into them.

Not only does this seem kind of pointless, but it is based on a misunderstanding of another of Paul's descriptions of the resurrection. The misunderstanding is understandable, given the years of baggage the centuries have added to our thinking. Here is the passage in question: "If we believe that Jesus died and rose again, even so God will bring with Him those who sleep in Jesus" (1 Thessalonians 4:14).

The assumption is that Jesus is rounding up the dead who live in heaven and will bring them back to earth when He returns. It's not a likely interpretation of the verse, however, given the fact that Paul describes the dead as "those who sleep in Jesus." They are not enjoying a conscious existence somewhere else in the universe. They are dead. When you read the verse in context, the difficulty disappears immediately:

> I do not want you to be ignorant, brethren, concerning those who have fallen asleep, lest you sorrow as others who have no hope. For if we believe that Jesus died and rose again, even so God will bring with Him those who sleep in Jesus.
>
> For this we say to you by the word of the Lord, that we who are alive and remain until the coming of the Lord will by no means precede those who are asleep. For the Lord Himself will descend from heaven with a shout, with the voice of an archangel, and with the trumpet of God. And the dead in Christ will rise first. Then we who are alive and remain shall be caught up together with them in the clouds to meet the Lord in the air. And thus we shall always be with the Lord. Therefore comfort one another with these words (verses 13–18).

The believers in Thessalonica were expecting Jesus to return, but they were worried about those who had died while waiting. Would they also be with Jesus, or was it "game over" for them? The fact that this is what they were worried about tells us something about their belief regarding death: they were afraid the dead were simply *gone*.

"Listen," Paul assures them, "I don't want you to be ignorant about how this will work. They are asleep right now, but don't forget that Jesus rose from the dead. Your friends are going to rise from the dead too. It's not just *you* who will go to heaven; God's going to bring the dead to heaven too."

Many people read this passage and conclude that Jesus brings the dead *from* heaven. But Paul is actually saying that one reason Jesus has come is to take the dead *to* heaven. In fact, the dead are raised *first*—before we leave with Jesus. Saving them is a high priority for Jesus, the One who Himself was once dead but is now alive forever.

We spend much time comforting each other by saying that the dead "are in a better place now." That isn't what the Bible tells us to say to comfort each other at the graveside. "Comfort one another with these words," says Paul. Which words? The ones that say the dead are asleep, but Jesus won't forget them when He comes.

This is phenomenal news! The grave doesn't have to be the end!

This explains what happens to those who accept the gift of salvation and repent of their sins. What happens to those who don't? What becomes of the wicked?

After a brief interlude, we'll examine what the Bible says about them.

Interlude

What's a *Soul*?

Perhaps no one thing has caused as much confusion on the topic of death and dying as the word *soul.* Much of that confusion has come from the way the King James translators used the word. We have come to think of the soul as the real you—a nonmaterial essence that inhabits your body and leaves when the body dies.

But while people may have gone off the track because of their misunderstanding of the King James Version's use of this word, the way that it is used the first time it appears in that version may do the most to provide the needed clarity: "The LORD God formed man of the dust of the ground, and breathed into his nostrils the breath of life; and man became a living soul" (Genesis 2:7).

Other translations simply say that man "became a living being." The Hebrew word that was translated "soul" in the King James Version is *nephesh,* which quite literally means "that which breathes," or "the breathing substance or being." It's a fuzzy word used to denote something that has life, but it doesn't mean *ghost.* Notice that the Bible says that man *be-came* a living soul; he didn't *receive* one.

In short, you do not *have* a soul; you *are* a soul. Most

modern translations say something to the effect that seventy *people* accompanied Jacob into Egypt. The King James Version tells us that "all the *souls* that came with Jacob into Egypt, which came out of his loins, besides Jacob's sons' wives, all the *souls* were threescore and six" (Genesis 46:26; emphasis added).

Likewise, the King James Version describes Abraham's departure from Haran this way: "Abram took Sarai his wife, and Lot his brother's son, and all their substance that they had gathered, and the *souls* that they had gotten in Haran; and they went forth to go into the land of Canaan; and into the land of Canaan they came" (Genesis 12:5; emphasis added). In both instances, the word *soul* has been translated from *nephesh,* and it is a clear reference to real, live, physical people, and not disembodied spirits.

Someone once claimed that the term *immortal soul* isn't found in the Bible and challenged me to prove him wrong. I took the challenge, but he was right; there is no such term anywhere in Scripture. There, only God is said to be immortal. He is the One "who alone has immortality" (1 Timothy 6:16). By contrast, we are told quite pointedly that human souls can die:

- "Behold, all souls are Mine; the soul of the father as well as the soul of the son is Mine; the soul who sins shall die" (Ezekiel 18:4).
- "The soul who sins shall die. The son shall not bear the guilt of the father, nor the father bear the guilt of the son. The righteousness of the righteous shall be upon himself, and the wickedness of the wicked shall be upon himself" (verse 20).

This, of course, is in perfect keeping with the assertion Paul makes in the book of Romans that the "wages of sin is death" (Romans 6:23). Unless you've received Jesus' gift of salvation, your soul can—and will—die because you have sinned. Your soul is not your ghost; your soul is *you*.

Chapter 6

The Fallen, the Wicked, and Hell

A young mother discovered that her little boy had lied to her. Utterly shocked and desperate to correct his wayward behavior, she sat him down and said to him, "Listen—you can't lie to Mommy! If you do that again, a big tall man with red eyes and horns is going to come and take you away. He'll make you work for a hundred years in the coal mines just for telling one little lie!"

The look on the boy's face told the mother that he was listening carefully. Encouraged that she was getting through to him, she said, "Now, you'll never lie to Mommy again, will you."

He thought for a moment and then blurted out, "No ma'am, I wouldn't dare—'cause you tell them better than I do!"

The Bible is crystal clear about what will happen to those who seek forgiveness and choose faith in Christ. They are given eternal life, which they'll spend in the presence of Christ. "The Lord Himself will descend from heaven with a shout, with the voice of an archangel, and with the trumpet of God. And the dead in Christ will rise first. Then we who are alive and remain shall be caught up together with them in the clouds to meet the Lord in the air. And thus we shall always be with the Lord" (1 Thessalonians 4:16, 17).

What happens to all the other people? Popular Christian literature says they'll suffer eternal torment in the fires of hell. Knowing that two thousand years of traditions and suppositions have accumulated since the Bible was completed, we need to ask whether or not it actually teaches such a notion. It's entirely possible that the pile of human assumptions has covered the simple biblical truth. Stories have been passed from generation to generation without the all-important step of scriptural verification. The nation of Israel went off the track of truth by absorbing the religious beliefs and practices of the Canaanites and the philosophies taught by the various nations that occupied their land. Is it possible that we've done the same?

Entirely. Consider this nineteenth-century account of the fate of the wicked, which a children's author named John Furniss (no pun intended—that was his name!) wrote to scare children into behaving.

> Come into this room. You see it is very small. But see, in the midst of it there is a girl, perhaps about eighteen years old. What a terrible dress she has on— her dress is made of fire. On her head she wears a bonnet of fire. It is pressed down close all over her head, it burns into the skin; it scorches the bone of the skull and makes it smoke. The red hot fiery heat goes into the brain and melts it. . . . There she will stand for ever burning and scorched! She counts with her fingers the moments as they pass away slowly, for each moment seems to her like a hundred years. As she counts the moments she remembers that she will have to count them for ever and ever.

> Look into this little prison. In the middle of it there is a boy, a young man. He is silent; despair is on him. He stands straight up. His eyes are burning like

two burning coals. Two long flames come out of his
ears. His breathing is difficult. Sometimes he opens
his mouth and a breath of blazing fire rolls out of it.
But listen! There is a sound just like that of a kettle
boiling! Is it really a kettle boiling? No; then what is
it? The blood is boiling in the scalded veins of that
boy. The brain is boiling and bubbling in his head.
The marrow is boiling in his bones. Ask him why he
is thus tormented. His answer is that when he was
alive, his blood boiled to do very wicked things.[1]

No such stories in the Bible

If you're searching the Bible for such vivid, stomach-
churning descriptions of the fate of the wicked, you'll be
searching in vain. The Bible has no lengthy, cruel descriptions
of children being tortured. In fact, it depicts children as the
special objects of Jesus' affection.

"But," you may ask, "doesn't the Bible teach that the
wicked are destined for fire?"

It does, in fact, teach something close to that. The fire,
according to the Bible, is quite real: "Anyone not found written in the Book of Life was cast into the lake of fire" (Revelation 20:15).

Case closed, right?

According to some Christians, Yes. But this statement is
brief and doesn't include much detail—and it certainly requires a lot of imaginative thinking to read John Furniss's fan-
tasy into it. All the Bible says is that the wicked—those whose
names are not found in the book of life—will be cast into the
lake of fire. That's the essence of it. Search for yourself and see.

That, frankly, is one key reason there are so many divergent
opinions within Christianity on so many topics: people fail to
read the whole Book. We seem to be very good at building a
case on a verse or two, when the picture presented *throughout*
Scripture would give a completely different scenario.

Suffice it to say, for the moment, that the concept of fire

for the wicked is very much present in the Bible. The question is whether or not the *entire* biblical picture matches the stories we were told as children. Is God a cruel tyrant who tortures people eternally when they don't agree with Him? Or is there more to what the Bible writers present as God's final dealings with evil?

The answer requires a bit of study. It's a bit of a jigsaw puzzle: many different Bible writers offer information, but each one gives us just a piece of two of the overall picture. It is tempting to gather just a few passages and base the conclusion on them. But if we do that, we will end up seeing only a small fraction of the picture. If, on the other hand, we assemble *all* of the pieces, we'll get remarkable clarity. God, it seems, is perfectly capable of speaking for Himself.

So far we've been able to determine that the Bible really *does* speak of fire for the wicked. But it also tells us that fire *wasn't meant for human beings.* That's right: it's not for us—at least, that wasn't the original plan. Most of the cartoons you've seen on the subject show devils with pitchforks poking and prodding human beings who have been damned to an eternity of suffering. But the biblical scheme doesn't place fallen angels in charge. In fact, when Jesus describes the people who will be lost in the end, He mentions that hell was meant for *fallen angels:* "Then He will also say to those on the left hand, 'Depart from Me, you cursed, into the everlasting fire prepared for the devil and his angels' " (Matthew 25:41).

The ramifications of this statement are huge. Not one human being was supposed to end up in the fires of hell! God didn't have us in mind when He came up with the scheme. Hell was meant for fallen angels. We will end up there only if we persist in giving our loyalty to them. *We end up in hell only because we follow the devil there.*

Which, of course, means that people *can* go to hell, but when they go there, it's because they chose to. Or, more accurately, people chose to go to the *fire,* because *hell* is a bit of a misnomer. Over the centuries, we've come to associate this word with a place that is reminiscent of the Canaanite abode of the dead—but with an element of brutal eternal torture added to it. When someone says "hell," we think of a fiery underworld where devils are in charge. Canaanites thought of Sheol as a shadowy realm where the gods of the underworld reigned. The Hebrews, of course, originally thought of Sheol as simply the grave.

When you read the word *hell* in the English Bible, it's a translation of one of several different Hebrew and Greek terms. The word *hell* appears more than fifty times in the King James Version. It appears less often in modern English translations—perhaps because translators began to recognize that the word *hell* can create confusion because it conjures up imagery that the Bible writers didn't intend to raise.

Sheol, Hades, and Gehenna

There are three key terms that have been translated as *hell,* one in Hebrew and the other two in Greek.

1. Sheol. To the ancient Hebrew mind, *Sheol* simply meant the grave. When David describes the omnipresence of God (His ability to be everywhere), he says, "Where can I go from Your Spirit? Or where can I flee from Your presence? If I ascend into heaven, You are there; If I make my bed in hell, behold, You are there" (Psalm 139:7, 8).

Did David expect God to hang out with him while he roasted in the fires of torment? Not only does that seem absurd, but it seems unlikely. God had said that David was a man after His own heart. It seems that a man so close to God wouldn't have been expecting to land in a place of eternal torment.

The word David used is *Sheol,* "the grave," and he was simply stating that even when he makes his bed in the grave, God will not abandon him. This is in perfect keeping, of course, with the imagery used throughout Scripture: death is a sleep; the grave is a bed.

In the sixteenth psalm, David prophetically anticipates the burial of Christ with a passage that Peter quoted in a sermon. In the King James Version, it reads like this: "Thou wilt not leave my soul in hell; neither wilt thou suffer thine Holy One to see corruption" (Psalm 16:10).

In the New King James Version—and other modern translations—the translators have, for the most part, chosen to leave the word untranslated: "You will not leave my soul in Sheol, nor will You allow Your Holy One to see corruption" (Psalm 16:10).

Jesus, of course, quite literally fulfilled this prophetic verse with the fact that He didn't remain in the grave but rose soon (three days) after He was placed there.

In a passage that we touched upon in a previous chapter, Job actually asks to be sent to Sheol, which, in the context, is obviously a reference to the grave—so translators have done us the service of translating *Sheol* as "grave." "Oh, that You would hide me in the grave [*Sheol*], that You would conceal me until Your wrath is past, that You would appoint me a set time, and remember me!" (Job 14:13).

It is doubtful that Job would have asked God to send him to a place of eternal torment. That would hardly provide the relief from suffering that he was seeking.

The fact that most of the Western world was pagan before Christianity arrived may have contributed to some of the baggage associated with the word *hell*. Like the Greeks, the Germanic tribes of northern Europe believed in a shadowy underworld, which was variously called *helle* (Frisian), *hel* (Dutch and Norse), *hölle* (German), or *halja* (Gothic). The word meant "the underworld" or "a concealed place." When translators used the word *hell* to convey the meaning of Sheol, the term was already fraught with the baggage of pagan mythology.*

2. Hades. The Greeks understood Hades in much the same way as the Canaanites understood Sheol; it was the shadowy underworld of the dead that lay beyond the river

---

* You can research the word on the *Online Etymology Dictionary,* at www.etymonline.com.

Styx. When the Bible uses the word, however, it is usually in reference to the grave. There is a striking example in the book of Acts, where Peter quotes Psalm 16, which we looked at earlier when we were discussing Sheol. The book of Acts, however, was written in Greek, so the word *Hades* is used: "You will not leave my soul in Hades, nor will You allow Your Holy One to see corruption" (Acts 2:27).

3. *Gehenna.* There is another Greek word that has been translated as *hell* in the New Testament, and it is important enough that it merits careful examination. The word is *Gehenna.* When this word is used, the meaning is more in line with our traditional concept of hell. The word was derived from *Hinnom,* which was the name of the valley just outside Jerusalem that served as a trash dump. As is the case at many modern trash dumps, the refuse people discarded there was burned.

When the Israelites were at their farthest from God and were engaging in the pagan rituals of the Canaanite tribes, they offered their own children as sacrifices to Moloch:

> Ahaz was twenty years old when he became king, and he reigned sixteen years in Jerusalem; and he did not do right in the sight of the LORD, as his father David had done. For he walked in the ways of the kings of Israel, and made molded images for the Baals. He burned incense in the Valley of the Son of Hinnom, and burned his children in the fire, according to the abominations of the nations whom the LORD had cast out before the children of Israel (2 Chronicles 28:1–3).

So, people had been burned in Gehenna, in the Valley of Hinnom. But in Jesus' day, people were not being tortured there. Rather, Gehenna was the place where trash was being burned up. We'll return to this later.

Thus far, we have discovered that the fires of hell are quite real, and that they were intended for fallen angels, not human beings. People will end up in the fire because they have chosen to persist in rebellion; they have chosen to follow the devil to his ultimate fate.

That fate, of course, is still in the future. The Bible doesn't teach that the wicked continue in conscious existence after they die. It teaches that, like the righteous dead, the wicked sleep in their graves—which means that the fire *isn't burning yet.*

Like a harvest

Perhaps the clearest picture of how the fire will work was presented in a parable Jesus told that compares the end of the world to a harvest:

> Another parable He put forth to them, saying: "The kingdom of heaven is like a man who sowed good seed in his field; but while men slept, his enemy came and sowed tares among the wheat and went his way. But when the grain had sprouted and produced a crop, then the tares also appeared. So the servants of the owner came and said to him, 'Sir, did you not sow good seed in your field? How then does it have tares?' He said to them, 'An enemy has done this.' The servants said to him, 'Do you want us then to go and gather them up?' But he said, 'No, lest while you gather up the tares you also uproot the wheat with them. Let both grow together until the harvest, and at the time of harvest I will say to the reapers, "First gather together the tares and bind them in bundles to burn them, but gather the wheat into my barn" ' " (Matthew 13:24–30).

There are lots of lessons to be gleaned (what other word could you possibly use for a harvest story?) from this parable, not the least of which is that we haven't been commissioned to separate the weeds, or tares, from the wheat. We aren't capable of judging who is part of God's harvest and who isn't. But this story also provides us with an important description of how God intends to use fire to carry out the verdict of the final judgment. To prevent any misunderstanding, Jesus continues by giving us a detailed explanation of the story He's told.

> He answered and said to them: "He who sows the good seed is the Son of Man. The field is the world, the good seeds are the sons of the kingdom, but the tares are the sons of the wicked one. The enemy who sowed them is the devil, the harvest is the end of the age, and the reapers are the angels. Therefore as the tares are gathered and burned in the fire, so it will be at the end of this age. The Son of Man will send out His angels, and they will gather out of His kingdom all things that offend, and those who practice lawlessness, and will cast them into the furnace of fire. There will be wailing and gnashing of teeth. Then the righteous will shine forth as the sun in the kingdom of their Father. He who has ears to hear, let him hear!" (verses 37–43).

Jesus leaves little room for misinterpretation. The harvest takes place at the end of the world, when the righteous and wicked are finally separated. Until then, they coexist in a field where the devil has corrupted God's originally perfect plan. At the end, however, the Son of Man separates the two groups, and the wicked end up in the fire.

This means, of course, that nobody is currently suffering in the fires of hell. If you've been worried that a loved one is suffering, put your mind at ease: there is no knowledge in the grave, no suffering, no pain, no conscious existence of any kind. The fire doesn't burn until after the Second Coming— which makes sense because final rewards are not given out until Jesus returns. Then He will say, "He who is unjust, let him be unjust still; he who is filthy, let him be filthy still; he who is righteous, let him be righteous still; he who is holy, let him be holy still. And behold, I am coming quickly, and My reward is with Me, to give to every one according to his work" (Revelation 22:11, 12).

One important question is *where* the wicked will be burned. Hollywood and cartoon artists usually place them in the bowels of the earth, in caverns of flowing lava. But of course, this idea is immediately suspect because of the way it resembles Greek mythology. The fact is that the Bible teaches no such thing.

In the apostle Paul's description of the Second Coming, he says the righteous dead rise from their graves and are caught up to meet Christ in the air (see 1 Thessalonians 4:13–18). They are taken to heaven, where Christ has prepared a place for them. Jesus said, "In My Father's house are many mansions; if it were not so, I would have told you. I go to prepare a place for you. And if I go and prepare a place for you, I will come again and receive you to Myself; that where I am, there you may be also" (John 14:2, 3). In other words, the righteous vacate the planet.

The wicked, however, are left behind. In fact, they don't come out of the grave at all during Jesus' second coming.* According to the book of Revelation, "the rest of the dead did not live again until the thousand years were finished" (Revelation 20:5).

The wicked live again

But at the close of the thousand years, the wicked will live again. They come back to life in what Jesus called the "resurrection of condemnation" (John 5:28). Daniel tells us they wake up to "shame and everlasting contempt" (Daniel 12:2). It's at this point that the fire falls on them, and we make a

* With the possible exception of notable offenders like Caiaphas. Jesus promised him that he would witness the Second Coming (see Matthew 26:64). Based on this assertion, many Bible scholars believe in something known as the "special resurrection," in which Caiaphas and others like him will be raised to see Jesus' return.

remarkable discover that *flies in the face of most everything we've ever been told!* "When the thousand years have expired, Satan will be released from his prison and will go out to deceive the nations which are in the four corners of the earth, Gog and Magog, to gather them together to battle, whose number [is] as the sand of the sea. They went up on the breadth of the earth and surrounded the camp of the saints and the beloved city. And fire came down from God out of heaven and devoured them" (Revelation 20:7–9).

Don't miss it: *hellfire devours the wicked.* It utterly consumes them. They don't flip and fry throughout the ceaseless ages of eternity. They aren't kept on a hotplate in never-ending, excruciating torment. The fire *devours* the wicked, and then the fire goes out. God doesn't torture people; if, ultimately, they don't want to be a part of His kingdom, He won't allow them to exist indefinitely, sinking to lower and lower depths of depravity. There is a limit to the pain and suffering that a God of love will allow. He waits. He is patient, hoping that more will elect to accept the gift of salvation. He is "longsuffering toward us, not willing that any should perish but that all should come to repentance" (2 Peter 3:9). But there *is* a limit. He can't wait forever. Sin *must* be abolished. Suffering *must* come to an end. And Christ *must* inherit the kingdom He won at Calvary.

When the fire does fall, it will devour the wicked. It will consume everything that leads to wickedness and causes pain. It will remove from existence everything that makes God's universe anything less than a God of love intended it to be. And then it will burn out.

But I thought . . .

I know. So did I—until I began allowing the Bible to speak for itself.

I had always thought the wicked would be screaming in a place of torment forever, without end. But the Bible doesn't teach anything of the sort. It presents a final fire that consumes and burns out. God's final promise is that He will "wipe away every tear from their eyes; there shall be no more death, nor sorrow, nor crying. There shall be no more pain, for the former things have passed away" (Revelation 21:4). That couldn't possibly be true if there were people somewhere in God's universe who were still experiencing pain.

The former things will pass away. The fire comes down from heaven on the surface of the earth and utterly consumes the wicked, and then it *goes out*. Don't take my word for it. Look carefully at some seldom-quoted passages of the Bible:

> "Behold, the day is coming, burning like an oven, and all the proud, yes, all who do wickedly will be stubble. And the day which is coming shall burn them up," says the LORD of hosts, "that will leave them neither root nor branch. But to you who fear My name the Sun of Righteousness shall arise with healing in His wings; and you shall go out and grow fat like stall-fed calves. You shall trample the wicked, for they shall be ashes under the soles of your feet on the day that I do this," says the LORD of hosts (Malachi 4:1–3).

Read it again, carefully. The wicked are not tormented eternally; they are consumed like dry grass. They are burned up. They are reduced to ashes.

- "You shall make them as a fiery oven in the time of Your anger; the LORD shall swallow them up in His wrath, and the fire shall devour them. Their offspring You shall destroy from the earth, and their descendants from among the sons of men" (Psalm 21:9, 10).
- "The wicked shall perish; and the enemies of the LORD, like the splendor of the meadows, shall vanish. Into smoke they shall vanish away" (Psalm 37:20).
- "The LORD preserves all who love Him, but all the wicked He will destroy" (Psalm 145:20).

I'm sure John Furniss meant well, but he was completely misguided. God doesn't torture stubbornly wicked people forever; He ends their existence. And He does it with the fire that was originally designed for the devil alone. Tragically, some people will insist on clinging to the fallen angels when they meet their fate, and this much is certain: the devil *will* be destroyed.

Ezekiel, in his classic description of the devil, not only chronicles his fall into iniquity, but he also describes his end: "You defiled your sanctuaries by the multitude of your iniquities, by the iniquity of your trading; therefore I brought fire from your midst; it devoured you, and I turned you to ashes upon the earth in the sight of all who saw you. All who knew you among the peoples are astonished at you; you have become a horror, and shall be no more forever" (Ezekiel 28:18, 19).

See? Even the *devil* is wiped out of existence in the final fire that cleanses the earth. So why do we think that the devil will be in charge of a place where he torments *us* for all eternity? The answer is simple: paganism. We bought the idea from the Greeks, the Babylonians, and the Canaanites. We certainly didn't get it from the Bible.

Untold damage has been done to the Christian cause by well-meaning preachers who have used the idea of God torturing people eternally. In addition to John Furniss, some of the best preachers in Christian history have mistakenly bought into the idea, going so far as to suggest that if wicked people were *not* being tortured, we couldn't possibly enjoy heaven.

For example, consider the words of the renowned preacher Jonathan Edwards. He said the view of the wicked being tormented in hell will be a font of happiness for the saints throughout eternity. Seeing their loved ones suffer will make paradise even more precious to them and will, in fact, increase their happiness![2]

And Samuel Hopkins, another prominent preacher of that time, said that the display of people who are suffering in hell reveals not only the divine character and glory, but it will also be "in favor of the redeemed, and most entertaining, and give the highest pleasure to those who love God, and [will] raise their happiness to ineffable heights. . . .

"Should it [this eternal punishment] cease, and this fire could be extinguished, it would, in a great measure, obscure the light of heaven, and put an end to a great part of the happiness and glory of the blessed."[3]

Really? It's hard to believe that God would entertain the righteous with the thought and/or sight of people frying in the fires of hell, especially when the Bible reveals God as saying, "I have no pleasure in the death of the wicked" (Ezekiel 33:11). I can understand why preachers would wrestle to make sense of an eternally burning hell; it seems completely out of character for a God of love. But instead of questioning the doctrine itself, they have attempted to establish a *reason* that it has to be so, and they have concluded that it must in some way heighten the enjoyment of those who are *not* there in hell.

But no such mental gymnastics are necessary. We don't have to apologize for God. The Bible doesn't teach an eternally burning hellfire.

Endnotes

1. Rev. J. Furniss, *Tracts for Spiritual Reading* (New York: P. J. Kenedy, 1877), 19. It is not insignificant that this tract is often quoted by atheists as an argument for abandoning Christianity.

2. Jonathan Edwards, "The Eternity of Hell Torments," in *Discourses on Various Important Subjects,* (1738); as quoted in "Quotes About Hell Fire From Christian Leaders," Tentmaker, accessed June 24, 2014, http://www.tentmaker.org/Quotes/hell-fire.htm.

3. Samuel Hopkins, *Works of Samuel Hopkins* (Boston: Doctrinal Tract and Book Society, 1852), 463, 470; as quoted in LeRoy Edwin Froom, *The Conditionalist Faith of Our Fathers* (Washington, D.C.: Review and Herald, 1965), 2:276.

Chapter 7

What About *Eternal* and *Forever?*

We have already considered several objections to what otherwise is a clear picture of what the Bible says it means to be dead. In this chapter, we'll look at two biblical ideas that seem to be totally incompatible with each other. The question is how we can believe both the clear biblical idea of a fire that burns out and the biblical passages that seem to state that it never will burn out. It seems that they can't both be true—the fire can't burn eternally *and* burn out. So how do we harmonize the two ideas?

One step toward harmonizing the two apparently incompatible beliefs is to understand the word *Gehenna,* which was a garbage dump outside the city of Jerusalem. It was not a place of torment but a place of destruction. Near the end of the nineteenth century, Dr. Lyman Abbott, a well-known Congregationalist minister and editor of the *Christian Union,* drew out the implications posed by this quite pointedly:

Outside the walls of Jerusalem, in the valley of

Gehenna, was kept perpetually burning a fire, on which the offal of the city was thrown to be destroyed. This is the hell fire of the New Testament. Christ warns his auditors that persistence in sin will make them offal to be cast out from the holy city, to be destroyed. The worm that dieth not was the worm devouring the carcasses, and is equally clearly a symbol not of torture but of destruction.[1]

Jesus often pointed to *Gehenna,* the garbage dump, when speaking about the fire that awaited the wicked, and He sometimes appears to be saying that the fire will burn forever: "If your hand causes you to sin, cut it off. It is better for you to enter into life maimed, rather than having two hands, to go to hell, into the fire that shall never be quenched—where 'Their worm does not die and the fire is not quenched' " (Mark 9:43, 44).

Some modern versions of the Bible have a footnote to indicate that the final phrase, "and the fire is not quenched," was not in the original manuscript. That would be a convenient way to explain the passage in light of the rest of what the Bible teaches regarding hell; but let's suppose, as I do, that Jesus actually spoke those words. It still makes sense—as long as you don't read a modern concept into the words. Jesus *appears* to be saying that the fire will never go out, but what He is really saying is that the fire cannot be *quenched,* which is quite different.

How so? A fire that burns eternally will *never* be put out. A fire that cannot be quenched cannot be *doused.* You cannot put it out until it has finished its job—until everything that's been put in the fire has been consumed. Not only was that the nature of the fire at *Gehenna,* the garbage dump, which burned day and night consuming trash, it was also the way God described the destruction of Jerusalem by Nebuchadnezzar:

"If you will not heed Me to hallow the Sabbath day,

such as not carrying a burden when entering the gates of Jerusalem on the Sabbath day, then I will kindle a fire in its gates, and it shall devour the palaces of Jerusalem, and it shall not be quenched" (Jeremiah 17:27).

When Israel refused to change her ways, the Babylonian army did, in fact, lay siege to the city of Jerusalem. The city *did* burn with a fire God called "unquenchable," and while it was burning, the personnel of the Jerusalem fire department found that they were powerless to quench it. However, it is quite evident that the fire didn't last forever. When it had done its work, it simply died out.

The same is true of the final fire—the one that destroys the wicked. Nobody will be able to stop it from doing its work. "Behold, they shall be as stubble, the fire shall burn them; they shall not deliver themselves from the power of the flame; it shall not be a coal to be warmed by, nor a fire to sit before!" (Isaiah 47:14).

When that fire falls, it will be too late to change your mind or alter your destiny. By the time Jesus returns, all decisions regarding people's relationship with Him will have been made. The righteous will remain righteous forever, and the wicked will remain wicked (Revelation 22:11). The wicked won't be able to deliver themselves from the fire. It will burn unquenchably until they become ashes. There is nothing in the concept of an unquenchable fire that disagrees with the rest of the data found in Scripture.

However, Jesus said something else that isn't as easy to reconcile: "Then He [God] will also say to those on the left hand, 'Depart from Me, you cursed, into the everlasting fire prepared for the devil and his angels' " (Matthew 25:41).

Again, it's probably apropos to point out that the fire wasn't intended for human beings. But there's also no escaping the fact that Jesus calls the fire "everlasting." This is a confusing claim in light of the numerous biblical passages in which the fire appears to burn out. When I first began to investigate the biblical picture of hell for myself, this verse repeatedly came to mind. So, my response was, "But Jesus said it was *'everlasting'*!"

Yes, He did. But the Bible also says that Sodom and Gomorrah were destroyed with "eternal" fire: "Sodom and Gomorrah, and the cities around them in a similar manner to these, having given themselves over to sexual immorality and gone after strange flesh, are set forth as an example, suffering the vengeance of eternal fire" (Jude 7).

Obviously, Sodom and Gomorrah are no longer burning. In fact, we're relatively certain that what's left of them is somewhere at the bottom of the Dead Sea. Why then does the Bible say they suffered "eternal fire"? Because it was the *results,* not the flames, that were eternal. Nobody ever rebuilt those cities. They will never come back. The work the fire did was once and for all. It was eternal. Likewise, the fire that falls on the wicked and devours them (Revelation 20:9) will do a once-and-for-all, permanent job. The wicked will not return after the fire has done its work. They will have been consumed, turned into smoke (Psalm 37:20), and they will never be back. Ever. Eternally.

God's final plan for the wicked

A study of God's final plan for the unrepentant underscores just how important it is to read the *entire* Bible in context. Christianity has been around for two thousand years now, and its various versions influence us, so it's easy to read our own philosophy into the text. But a broad, exhaustive reading usually helps us to discern what the authors intended when they used certain terms.

That certainly applies to the one remaining "problem" text that seems to contradict the idea that the fire is eventually extinguished: "The devil, who deceived them, was cast into the lake of fire and brimstone where the beast and the false prophet are. And they will be tormented day and night forever and ever" (Revelation 20:10).

This is perhaps the most difficult text to reconcile because it mentions torment that goes on "day and night forever and ever." Yet elsewhere the Bible promises that God intends to re-create the earth. "Behold, I create new heavens and a new earth," God says (Isaiah 65:17). And centuries later, Peter wrote that "we, according to His promise, look for new heavens and new earth" (2 Peter 3:13). This world will eventually be re-created and become our home—which poses an interesting problem. If fire falls on the wicked on *this earth* (Revelation 20:9) and God intends to take up residence with us on this earth (Revelation 21:1–3), how can the wicked be tormented on this earth *without ceasing*?

The answer lies in the Bible's use of the term *forever*. We think of "forever" as something that never, ever ends. But in the Bible, it is used for an experience that lasts as long as the person or object going through that experience lasts. So if I say that something lasts forever, I might mean that it lasts as long as I do, or that the experience will continue, uninterrupted, until it has run its intended course. It's like unquenchable fire—it lasts until it has done its job; nobody can disrupt it.

This may be a little confusing, but here are some clear biblical examples that make the point. The first one is from the story of Samuel: "Hannah did not go up [to Shiloh], for she said to her husband, 'Not until the child is weaned; then I will take him, that he may appear before the LORD and remain there forever' " (1 Samuel 1:22).

Hannah promised that Samuel would serve in Shiloh "forever." However, not only is Samuel dead now, but Shiloh is no longer the center of worship in Israel.

A few verses later, Hannah defines exactly what she meant by "forever": "I also have lent him to the LORD; as long as he lives he shall be lent to the LORD" (verse 28).

So, how long was Hannah's "forever"? As long as Samuel lived.

Another great illustration of the biblical use of *forever* comes from the book of Jonah. When the reluctant prophet is describing his ordeal in the belly of the fish, he says, "I went down to the moorings of the mountains; the earth with its bars closed behind me forever; yet You have brought up my life from the pit, O LORD, my God" (Jonah 2:6).

In a single sentence, Jonah tells us both that the experience lasted forever *and* that God had ended it. So, which is it?

It's both. Jonah's experience in the fish lasted *forever* in the sense that it continued until God's purpose was accomplished. In the Bible, *forever* doesn't necessarily mean "without end." That conclusion is certainly true regarding the destruction of the wicked. When the fire falls, it will do a complete work. The wicked will be utterly destroyed, never to return. They are not tortured forever; it's the smoke of their torment that "ascends forever and ever" (Revelation 14:11).

In other words, the results of the fire are permanent. Sin and suffering are over, never to return. "What do you conspire against the LORD?" the prophet Nahum once asked. "He will make an utter end of it. Affliction will not rise up a second time" (Nahum 1:9).

Perhaps the clearest statement on the fate of the wicked is found in the most famous passage in the Bible. "For God so loved the world that He gave His only begotten Son, that whoever believes in Him should not perish but have everlasting life. For God did not send His Son into the world to condemn the world, but that the world through Him might be saved" (John 3:16, 17).

Read through that several times. Let the words sink in. The righteous inherit eternal life, but the wicked *perish*. It doesn't say that they have a different sort of eternal life—a brutal one, in hellfire. It doesn't say they will be tortured eternally. It says they will *perish*.

God isn't a monster. His deepest desire is to get people *into* the kingdom, not to keep people out. He didn't send His Son into the world to condemn the world but to save it. He's not trying to lose you. He has given everything He could possibly give—including His own life—in order to secure your place in His kingdom.

God loves you. He's not a vindictive God who tortures people who disagree; He's a merciful God who ultimately puts a suffering world out of its misery. He doesn't force anybody to love Him. He doesn't coerce anybody into the kingdom, because that wouldn't be love. But He also cannot bear the thought that the pain and suffering we have caused in our rebellion against Him will go on forever, getting worse by the century, by the millennium.

At some point, God draws a line in the sand and declares that the suffering must stop. Those who persist in sin will simply be stopped from making things any worse.

And what of those who accept the gift of Christ's sacrifice at the cross? "God will wipe away every tear from their eyes; there shall be no more death nor sorrow, nor crying. There shall be no more pain, for the former things have passed away" (Revelation 21:4).

Endnote

1. Lyman Abbott, "There Is Very Little in the New Testament to Warrant Belief in Endless Conscious Sin and Suffering; Much in It Showing That the End of Sin Is Absolute Death," in *That Unknown Country* (Springfield, MA: C. A. Nichols, 1888), 72.

Chapter 8

The Next World

Perhaps the most striking aspect of the Bible's portrayal of the afterlife is just how real it is. Human beings never were ethereal spirits, and they—we—are not destined to spend eternity, or any portion of it, as ghosts. The Greeks and other pagan cultures neatly divided our existence into two parts, the physical and the spiritual, but the Bible describes us as individual, whole beings made up of the physical as well as the spiritual.

In spite of the present fascination with the supernatural, as evidenced by the popularity of TV shows such as *Ghost Hunters,* modern people struggle to come to grips with a religion that seems ethereal and altogether otherworldly. The realm of departed souls doesn't appear to have much to do with our present existence. That realm is "out there" somewhere, and if it exists, we'll deal with it later when we die. But for now, we have real living to do—living in the physical world.

This division of life into two parts—the present, physical life and the future spiritual life—comes from pagan mythology, not biblical anthropology. A good Greek philosopher would have spurned physical existence as imperfect and therefore something to be rid of as quickly as possible. So would the later Gnostics, who imported such notions directly into the early heresies of the Christian church.* But the Bible reveals a God who created material people, placed them in a physical world, and then smiled as He declared His creation to be "very good" (Genesis 1:31).

Like the Greeks and other dualists, Christians sense that something is wrong with creation. However, we don't attribute it to some sort of flaw inherent in material existence. Instead, we attribute it to the damage done to God's perfect creation by our rebellion. The universe is marred, and our existence is brutal, because we have made it that way by an act of treason against the Creator.

The remarkable thing about it is the persistent love of the Creator. He intends to restore creation to what it was, and He insists on giving back everything we gave away. You will notice that the Bible begins with the human race being escorted out of the Garden, doomed to live under a curse (Genesis 3:14–24). The story moves immediately from Creation to the Fall—to the point when our lives became difficult, when our existence was a matter of living by the sweat of our brow until we return to the dust of the ground.

But the Bible ends with that curse being lifted and the Garden restored:

> "Behold, I create new heavens and a new earth; and the former shall not be remembered or come to mind" (Isaiah 65:17).

> Now I saw a new heaven and a new earth, for the first heaven and the first earth had passed away.

---

* The Gnostic sects held material existence in such disdain that they attributed Creation to a demiurge, a lesser god, who simply got things wrong. Jesus, they said, had to come and fix things for the Creator and reveal ways for us to escape the prison of our imperfect material existence.

Also there was no more sea. Then I, John, saw the holy city, New Jerusalem, coming down out of heaven from God, prepared as a bride adorned for her husband. And I heard a loud voice from heaven saying, "Behold, the tabernacle of God is with men, and He will dwell with them, and they shall be His people. God Himself will be with them and be their God. And God will wipe away every tear from their eyes; there shall be no more death, nor sorrow, nor crying. There shall be no more pain, for the former things have passed away" (Revelation 21:1–4).

And he showed me a pure river of water of life, clear as crystal, proceeding from the throne of God and of the Lamb. In the middle of its street, and on either side of the river, was the tree of life, which bore twelve fruits, each tree yielding its fruit every month. The leaves of the tree were for the healing of the nations. And there shall be no more curse, but the throne of God and of the Lamb shall be in it, and His servants shall serve Him. They shall see His face, and His name shall be on their foreheads (Revelation 22:1–4).

There is nothing ethereal about it. The Holy City descends onto this planet, which has been completely restored after the wicked have been put out of their misery. God is rebuilding a *real* home for us, another Eden, populated by *real* people engaged in *real* lives—except the things that plague us most will no longer be present.

The natural world restored

The natural world will be restored to its former glory. The pestilences that rob us of our peace of mind, the droughts that threaten our food supply, the diseases that rob us of the joy of living, the crimes that cheat us of our living—they'll all be gone.

The wilderness and the wasteland shall be glad for them, and the desert shall rejoice and blossom as the rose; it shall blossom abundantly and rejoice, even with joy and singing. The glory of Lebanon shall be given to it, the excellence of Carmel and Sharon. They shall see the glory of the LORD, the excellency of our God.

Strengthen the weak hands, and make firm the feeble knees. Say to those who are fearful-hearted, "Be strong, do not fear! Behold, your God will come with vengeance, with the recompense of God; He will come and save you."

Then the eyes of the blind shall be opened, and the ears of the deaf shall be unstopped. Then the lame shall leap like a deer, and the tongue of the dumb sing. For waters shall burst forth in the wilderness, and streams in the desert. The parched ground shall become a pool, and the thirsty land springs of water; in the habitation of jackals, where each lay, there shall be grass with reeds and rushes (Isaiah 35:1–6).

"They shall build houses and inhabit them; they shall plant vineyards and eat their fruit. They shall not build and another inhabit; they shall not plant and another eat; for as the days of a tree, so shall be the days of My people, and My elect shall long enjoy the work of their hands. They shall not labor in vain, nor bring forth children for trouble; for they shall be the descendants of the blessed of the LORD, and their offspring with them.

"It shall come to pass that before they call, I will answer; and while they are still speaking, I will hear. The wolf and the lamb shall feed together, the lion shall eat straw like the ox, and dust shall be the serpent's food. They shall not hurt nor destroy in all My holy mountain," says the LORD (Isaiah 65:21–25).

Read those passages through again. In fact, read them several times. Get a highlighter or a red pen and mark them. Notice the way that everything that plagues us will be utterly turned upside down.

- The cruelty of diseases and disabilities will be a thing of the past. The ravages of aging will be reversed. Even now we can face the onset of age with confidence, knowing that it is but the temporary effect of living in this present damaged world. When the new world comes, it will never happen again. Our faltering eyes will become sharp, our degenerating joints and disks fully restored.
- Scarcity—the cause of so many wars and acts of cruelty—will be over. Water will flow in the desert. The wilderness will blossom. There will be no need for sponsors to feed starving children and no need to wonder how we will survive when we retire.
- After a lifetime of virtual slavery, working for someone else (or, if you're self-employed, working for the tax department), we will enjoy the works of our hands. Of course, everything we do will be done to the glory of the Creator, and He will own everything. But we know He understands the satisfaction we feel in creativity and accomplishment because we were made in His image. We will be permitted to enjoy the things that bring us the deepest satisfaction and bring the highest honor to His name.
- Even the wildlife will enjoy the new epoch of peaceful existence. Our sin took a toll on the whole planet, changing the entire order of existence for all of God's creatures. There even came a point when the fear of human beings had to be instilled into the members of the animal kingdom (see Genesis 9:2). When God

restores His creation, it will all be reversed. We will never have to wonder if a dog is about to attack us or if it is safe for our children to play in the woods. Pain, suffering, and death are finished!

It's hard to imagine, isn't it? It's so unlike the world we presently live in. Perhaps that's the reason we became attracted to the notion that the afterlife must be immaterial. We could imagine no other way to be rid of the things that bedevil us most.

A better answer

How can we live in our world without feeling hunger or pain? The Greeks said the answer is to get rid of our bodies. There is some allure to their way of thinking—except that instinctively we know that an ethereal, ghostly existence is not human. It wouldn't be satisfying because we weren't designed to live that way.

There's a reason those passages from Isaiah stir deep emotions: they speak to our deepest needs. There is a memory of Eden in every human heart—which is the reason we find our present existence so problematic. We instinctively remember something better.

The good news: the next life is real. There is no mention of floating on clouds with harps; no mention of ghostly apparitions or mysterious realms in which there is no physical existence. We live, we work, we build, and we enjoy. It's all explained in very real terms for a very real, physical future.

And in the center of the story, between paradise lost and paradise regained, is the real death of another real human being, the God-man Jesus Christ. In assuming human form, He became as real as you and me. And when He returns, He will come as a real, flesh-and-blood human being. He rose from the dead with a physical body—one that could be touched; one that could eat fish and honeycomb (Luke 24:38–42). This "same Jesus" is the One who returns to close up earth's rebellious phase and to usher in His own kingdom (Acts 1:11).

He is as physically real as you are. He understands what it means to live in this place, to suffer pain and rejection and loneliness. He has been hungry and sleep deprived. He has faced the injustice of a human court stacked with self-interested pretenders who ranked their own agendas higher than honesty and fairness. He has been ruthlessly mocked, run out of town, and misunderstood. He is the perfect Mediator, the perfect Representative to stand in heaven at the head of the human race. "For we do not have a High Priest who cannot sympathize with our weaknesses, but was in all points tempted as we are, yet without sin. Let us therefore come boldly to the throne of grace, that we may obtain mercy and find grace to help in time of need" (Hebrews 4:15, 16).

The Bible is a real story for real people. While it certainly does deal in grand themes that challenge our ability to comprehend, it isn't speaking of concepts that exist only in an esoteric world of ether. Scripture deals with real, flesh-and-blood people who face real, life-and-death issues. It's a good guide for people who have to face the real world now, and it's an incredible source of hope for people who long for the real world when they face death.

I don't know about you, but I could use that kind of miracle.

Chapter 9

Negative Influences and Positive Witnesses

It can be difficult to read through the Bible objectively, given the way that so many folktales and traditions have been added to the Christian system of belief over the years. In addition to the Greek culture that influenced the nation of Israel, we have inherited a number of superstitions from the unfortunate ignorance of the medieval period, appropriately called the Dark Ages. This period is usually considered dark because the classical learning of ancient Western civilizations—the Greeks and the Romans—was all but lost after the barbarian conquest of Rome. Civilization quite literally unraveled in the western half of the Roman Empire, especially after A.D. 476—after the Roman government, under Justinian, retreated to Constantinople in the east, and the religious governance of the western half of the empire was entrusted to the bishop of Rome. The Roman prelate's influence over the princes of Europe was unmistakable.

The loss of classical learning in areas such as philosophy, engineering, and science produced a vacuum of knowledge that was often filled by superstition and a distinctly dualistic worldview. The church—well steeped in the Roman worldview, thanks to the endorsement of Christianity by Constantine—gave western Europe a dualistic worldview. This was easily accepted, of course, by people whose background was Germanic paganism.

This period of Europe's history was a rough one, complete with brutal pandemics and bloody invasions by Vikings and Muslims. It certainly confirmed Thomas Hobbes's observation (which I noted back in chapter 2) that in the absence of civilization, human existence is "solitary, poor, nasty, brutish and short."[1] As we would expect, people longed to make sense of their brutal existence, so they readily absorbed superstitious notions as a means of explaining their world and the human condition.

Some of the traditions that made their way into Christendom were relatively harmless: Black cats were said to be evil spirits that could sever your connection with God simply by crossing your path. Breaking a mirror could prove to be bad luck, not only because mirrors were so expensive but also because a reflection was somehow representative of your soul. Knocking on wood for good luck had once been a nod to the spirits of the trees; it was later baptized into Christianity by associating the wood with the cross. Ladders were used to retrieve bodies from the gallows; so it was easy to be persuaded that the spirits of the hanged congregated under ladders, which made walking under ladders bad luck.

There was an element of dualism in most of these pagan traditions that found easy acceptance in a Dark Ages Christianity that had been heavily influenced by the sun-worshiping pagan convert Constantine. Tossing salt over one's shoulder or hanging a horseshoe over one's door may have supported spiritualistic superstition, but these actions didn't directly influence one's understanding of death and dying. Other traditions, however—such as the widespread notions that people become angels after death and that the dead must burn off their imperfections in purgatory before being admitted into an ethereal paradise—had a deeper and more consequential influence and continue to be a part of people's thinking about death even in our day.

Besides two thousand years of superstitious baggage, we also come to the topis of death and dying with strong emotions. It's hard to be objective, because the subjects can be so painful. Few of us have not had the profound impact of the loss of someone close, and some already live in the shadow of the Grim Reaper because they've been told they're dying.

These factors make it all the more necessary for us to sit quietly with a Bible and ask ourselves what it's actually saying and what it's not saying. It's truly remarkable how many of our forerunners in the Christian faith have done just that and have come away convinced that our belief system has been tainted by nonbiblical thinking.*

The church acts

It isn't insignificant that in 1513, the church, still emerging from the Dark Ages, issued a bull (an official pronunciation) against those who were suggesting that the human soul was not immortal.[2] The fact that the leaders of the church

---

* LeRoy Froom's *The Conditionalist Faith of Our Fathers* is a two-volume set that contains hundreds upon hundreds of pages of testimonies by dedicated Christian thinkers who managed to shed the medieval superstitions they had held about death by studying what the Bible actually teaches on this subject. The books are now out of print, but you may be able to find them on eBay or some other such place. They're likely to be pricey, but they're worth having (almost) no matter the price.

Conditionalists are people who believe in "conditional immortality." In other words, they believe that human beings are not naturally immortal; they become immortal only when God makes them so after the resurrection.

apparently felt the need to take such action reveals that growing numbers of believers were discovering the biblical picture of death. Among those making the discovery was Martin Luther, the great champion of righteousness by faith and one of the early Reformers. Luther noticed, on more than one occasion, the biblical teaching that the dead don't have a conscious existance but are merely asleep. His belief regarding death was what led him to question the teachings of purgatory and the worship of departed saints. Consider this passage from 1542:

> We Christians, who have been redeemed from all this through the precious blood of God's Son, should train and accustom ourselves in faith to despise death and regard it as a deep, strong, sweet sleep; to consider the coffin as nothing other than a soft couch of ease or rest. As verily, before God, it truly is just this; for he testifies, John 11:11: Lazarus our friend sleeps; Matthew 9:24: The maiden is not dead, she sleeps.
>
> Thus, too, St. Paul in 1 Corinthians 15, removes from sight all hateful aspects of death as related to our mortal body and brings forward nothing but charming and joyful aspects of the promised life. He says there (vv. 42ff.): It is sown in corruption and will rise in incorruption; it is sown in dishonor (that is, a hateful, shameful form) and will rise in glory; it is sown in weakness and will rise in strength; it is sown in a natural body and will rise a spiritual body.[3]

William Tyndale produced one of the first English translations of the Bible, and he also recognized the Bible's perspective that death is like sleep. In 1529, Sir Thomas More objected to Luther's doctrine that "all souls lie and sleep till doomsday."[4] Tyndale, in his *Answer to Sir Thomas More's*

Dialogue, defended it vigorously as the doctrine not only of Luther but of the Bible. He responded to the condemnation with a statement that demonstrates his understanding that medieval Christianity had been contaminated by pagan philosophy:

> Ye, in putting them [departed souls] in heaven, hell, and purgatory, destroy the arguments wherewith Christ and Paul prove the resurrection. . . . The true faith putteth [sets forth] the resurrection, which we be warned to look for every hour. The heathen philosophers, denying that, did put [set forth] that the souls did ever live. And the pope joineth the spiritual doctrine of Christ and the fleshly doctrine of philosophers together; things so contrary that they cannot agree, no more than the Spirit and the flesh do in a christian [*sic*] man. . . . And again, if the souls be in heaven, tell me why they be not in as good case as the angels be? And then what cause is there of the resurrection?[5]

The English poet John Milton is perhaps best known for his work *Paradise Lost,* in which he chronicles, albeit it fancifully and poetically, the journey of the devil and his angels, and then the human race, through the fall into rebellion and sin. In another, less poetical work, he weighs in on the biblical understanding of human beings in death:

> Inasmuch then as the whole man is uniformly said to consist of body, spirit, and soul (whatever may be the distinct provinces assigned to these divisions), I will show, that in death, first, the whole man, and secondly, each component part suffers privation of life. . . .
> The grave is the common guardian of all till the day of judgment.[6]

In 1683, John Tillotson, the archbishop of Canterbury, made the telling admission that the doctrine of the "immortality of the soul was rather supposed, or taken for granted, than expressly revealed in the Bible."[7]

In 1896, William Gladstone, prime minister of Britain and an able theologian, pinpointed one of the persons most responsible for bringing the notion of immortal souls into Judeo-Christian belief—Origen of Alexandria.

> It seems to me as if it were from the time of Origen that we are to regard the idea of natural, *as opposed to that of Christian,* immortality as beginning to gain a firm foothold in the Christian Church. . . .
>
> The doctrine of natural, as distinguished from Christian, immortality had not been subjected to the severer tests of wide publicity and resolute controversy, *but had crept into the Church, by a back door as it were;* by a silent though effective process; and was in course of obtaining a title by tacit prescription. . . .
>
> Another consideration of the highest importance is that *the natural immortality of the soul is a doctrine wholly unknown to the Holy Scriptures,* and standing on no higher plane than that of an ingeniously sustained, but gravely and formidably contested, philosophical opinion. . . .
>
> The character of the Almighty is rendered liable to charges which cannot be repelled so long as the idea remains that there may by His ordinance be such a thing as never-ending punishment, but that it will have been sufficiently vindicated at the bar of human judgment, so soon as it has been established and allowed that punishment, whatever else it may be, cannot be never-ending.[8]

A more recent proponent

Another well-known proponent of the biblical position on death as sleep was Dr. Emil Brunner, who served as professor of systematic theology at the University of Zurich and as a guest professor at Princeton. He openly admitted the influence of Greek paganism on Christian thought:

> Widely spread among all peoples and at all times is the idea of a survival of the soul after death, i.e. the view that death means the separation of soul from body. This view appears in many varied forms, *from primitive animism* to the philosophical doctrine of immortality. It assumes the form of the *Indian teaching* of Karma about the reincarnation of the soul in another life in a state corresponding to its ethical worth. Again it appears in the idea, first found in ancient *Egypt,* of an other-worldly judgment, in which some souls will be assigned to a joyful and radiant world, others to a dark, joyless, and tormented existence in the beyond. . . .
>
> For the history of Western thought, the Platonic teaching of the immortality of the soul became of special significance. It penetrated so deeply into the thought of Western man because, although with certain modifications, it was assimilated by Christian theology and church teaching, [it] was even declared by the Lateran Council of 1512 [1513] to be a dogma, to contradict which was a heresy, and likewise from Calvin onwards it was assumed in post-Reformation Protestantism to be a part of Christian doctrine. Only recently, as a result of a deepened understanding of the New Testament, have strong doubts arisen as to its compatibility with the Christian conception of the relation between God and man, and its essentially pre-Christian origin has been ever more emphasized.[9]

Brunner was quite right: the idea that our souls leave our bodies at death is quite at odds with the biblical understanding of our relationship to God. If we are essentially spirit beings, what is the point of a physical existence at all? In the same passage, Brunner goes on to point out that if Plato (and by extension, the Greeks) are right, then death isn't much of a problem at all. It really can't hurt you. And if nobody *really* dies, then the Bible is making too much of a fuss of it. That, of course, is the point on which the devil first tempted Eve.

> Now the serpent was more cunning than any beast of the field which the LORD God had made. And he said to the woman, "Has God indeed said, 'You shall not eat of every tree of the garden'?" And the woman said to the serpent, "We may eat the fruit of the trees of the garden; but of the fruit of the tree which [is] in the midst of the garden, God has said, 'You shall not eat it, nor shall you touch it, lest you die.' " Then the serpent said to the woman, "You will not surely die. For God knows that in the day you eat of it your eyes will be opened, and you will be like God, knowing good and evil" (Genesis 3:1–5).

"You will not surely die," the serpent whispered, and we've been listening ever since. Nearly every religious belief system known to the human race has taught the same lie: You *don't* surely die. You go on. Your soul is recycled, or it ascends to a higher place. But you don't really die.

Since that time, fallen angels have preyed on our worst fears and cashed in on the pagan superstition that has infiltrated our thinking. They make things go bump in the night. They speak with the voice and mannerisms of loved ones who have been ripped away from us by death. They continue whispering that we do not surely die. But be assured that God knew what He was talking about. You can safely ignore the voices, because God has told us that the dead do not speak and that death is real.

If we dismiss the idea that death actually means a total cessation of life, we effectively diminish the seriousness of sin. The Bible teaches that the "wages of sin is death"; it is not a conscious existence in some other realm. We do not merely cross an invisible barrier into the spirit world. We actually *cease to exist*. We are lost to God's universe.

It is no small wonder that Jesus shuddered in the Garden of Gethsemane when He faced the prospect of death. It is telling that He felt Himself so completely separated from the presence of God that He begged, "Let this cup pass from Me," and He cried out, "My God, My God, why have You forsaken Me?" (Matthew 26:39; Matthew 27:46). He understood death better than Socrates did. You can't go on living indefinitely apart from God. Without His atoning sacrifice, the human race was lost. Forever.

And because Jesus knew what sin would do to us, He gave His life to make sure that we could be reunited with the Creator. His death was quite real so that our eternal lives can be quite real too. There is no need to be confused about what happened at the cross, to let pagan mythology blur the lines between His life and His death. We can safely drain the river Styx and remove the mystery. There is no ferry to ride, no toll to pay.

Be assured that Jesus really died, and He really lives. And there is no need to be perplexed about what *your* future holds; no need to let Plato confuse the line between your life and death. You will—if Jesus doesn't return before the moment comes—really die. And then you will really live.

It is high time for us to shed the superstition of centuries and embrace the beautiful sacrificial majesty of what Jesus actually purchased for us at Calvary.

Endnotes

1. Thomas Hobbes, "Of the Naturall Condition of Mankind," in *Leviathan* (London: Andrew Crooke, 1651).

2. Henry J. Schroeder, *Disciplinary Decrees of the General Councils: Text, Translation, and Commentary* (St. Louis, MO: B. Herder, 1937), 16; as quoted in LeRoy Edwin Froom, *The Conditionalist Faith of Our Fathers* (Washington, DC: Review and Herald, 1965), 2:61.

3. Martin Luther, *Christian Songs Latin and German, for Use at Funerals,* in *Works of Luther* (Philadelphia: A. J. Holman, 1932), 6:287, 288; as quoted in Froom, 2:77.

4. See Froom, 2:94.

5. William Tyndale, *An Answer to Sir Thomas More's Dialogue* (Cambridge: Cambridge University Press, 1850; Parker's 1850 reprint), bk. 4, 180, 181.

6. John Milton, *The Prose Works of John Milton,* trans. Charles R. Sumner (London: George Bell and Sons, 1887), 4:271, 280, 281; as quoted in Froom, 2:154, 158.

7. John Tillotson, *The Works of the Most Reverend Mr. John Tillotson* (London: Goodwin, Trook, and Pemberton, 1817), 1:749; as quoted in Froom, 2:193.

8. William Gladstone, *Studies Subsidiary to the Works of Bishop Butler* (Oxford: Clarendon Press, 1896), 184, 195, 197, 241; all emphasis has been added to the original text; as quoted in Froom, 2:631, 634, 635.

9. Emil Brunner, *Eternal Hope* (Philadelphia: Westminster Press, 1954), 100; as quoted in Froom, 2:895, 896.

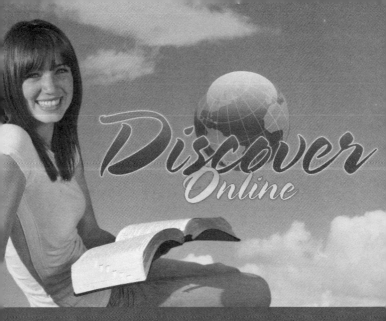

FREE Lessons at www.BibleStudies.com

Call:
1-888-456-7933

Write:
Discover
P.O. Box 2525
Newbury Park, CA 91319

It's easy to learn more about the Bible!